SPRING IN ALDGATE

Returning to the crowded and vibrant world of the East End, Ralph L. Finn adds a fresh bunch of colourful characters and memorable episodes to those recounted in the first volume of his autobiography, *No Tears in Aldgate*.

Here, side by side with the unforgettable contemporaries of his boyhood, comes a variety of saints and sinners—priest and prostitute, virgin and virago, millionaire and market man—so that the book brims with an exuberance and excitement of lovable villains.

Finn recreates a way of life now gone. Those who knew and loved the East End as it was will recognize it from this affectionate picture; those who didn't will be enthralled by these sometimes funny, sometimes solemn, recollections of one who grew up there.

SPRING IN ALDGATE

RALPH L. FINN

A New Portway Book

CHIVERS PRESS
BATH

First published in Great Britain 1968
by
Robert Hale Limited
This edition published
by
Chivers Press
by arrangement with
Robert Hale Limited
at the request of
The London & Home Counties Branch
of
The Library Association
1987

ISBN 0 86220 568 9

British Library Cataloguing in Publication Data

Finn, Ralph L.
  Spring in Aldgate.—(A New Portway book).
  1. Tower Hamlets (London, England)—
  Social life and customs
  I. Title
  942.1′5083′0924   DA685.T78

ISBN 0–86220–568–9

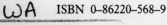
Printed and bound in Great Britain by
Redwood Burn Ltd, Trowbridge, Wiltshire

When I wrote *No Tears in Aldgate* some reviewers were quick to notice that the only character who did not really come alive was my mother. It was very perceptive of them. And the reason was plain: she was still alive. She was alive —a wonderful, mentally alert old woman in the mid-eighties —even as I wrote this book. But just before its publication she died, leaving an emptiness in me which will never be filled. She may not come alive in these pages but her spirit breathes through the book and it is to her I dedicate it thus:

TO MY MOTHER

whose memory will never die

Awake and sing all ye that dwell in dust
Isaiah

Contents

Prologue

Since the publication of *No Tears in Aldgate* I have been moved by the steady flow of letters from all over the world: warm, evocative, nostalgic letters praising the book and asking for more.

When John Mather, who had inspired the first book, died, I thought his death should not go unsung. In the sadness at his passing was born another book—this book, in which I have tried to echo some of the fun of past days and through which I have sought to recreate the joy in living that made the East End unique in the days between the wars.

Most of the characters who crowd these pages are, alas, dead now. The war took its toll of the more active ones, a bomb, smack on the buildings, accounted for most of the stay-at-homes and old age caught up with the few who survived. They are dead, most of the riotous ones who lived life so rumbustiously and used to be so very much alive. But the aliveness of their spirit is indestructible. I hope I have captured some of that joyous indestructibility in the pages that follow.

LONDON   R.L.F.
SEPTEMBER 1968

When I was a Child

MY FATHER died when I was three. I was five when we moved into Broughton Buildings. We came from a ten-roomed house in Tenter Street, where the early Dutch seamen, mostly retired captains, had settled in style and in which district, later, the more affluent Jewish families had also set up home. Tenter Street—the Tenterground, as it was known—was only down two roads from Broughton Buildings; but it was many roads up on the plane of existence. We slipped downhill.

We moved into two flats in Broughton Street, two two-roomed flats, each complete with scullery and lavatory. It was not Tenter Street but, compared with the way many others lived, it was still luxury. We had come down in the world, but I was not aware of it. Broughton Buildings became my home for the next twelve or thirteen years of my life. I was formed, you might say, by the Buildings.

I played alone as a child. I was still speaking a puzzling language, a hotchpotched mixture of English and Yiddish —the result of having been brought up in a bilingual home —and I must have seemed strange to the other children.

Maybe I was strange, too. For I played one of the most fantastic games any child could ever have played. I played it alone. I can only call it The Bell Game now. I had no name for it then.

I always seemed to play it on hot still days when the East End, tired by the sun, did not seem to have the energy to rouse itself to its normal pitch of noise. I played it on Saturday afternoons when the streets were empty and the air, heavy with heat, hung like velvet over the quiet streets and draped the grey tenements, stifling air and sound.

Somewhere in the City a bell used to chime. It might have been a church bell. It might have been just a clock that went on sounding its bell-like peals. One only heard it plainly when the East End was quiet and the days were hot and life slowed down to a whisper.

Then, on the still air, around the East End streets, the distant bells could be heard, chiming, chiming, chiming. I heard them. As a five-year-old I heard them.

I went towards the sound. It became louder. I walked away from it. The sound grew fainter. I walked on till the sound was no more, till, straining my sensitive young ears, I could not hear it at all. Stop. Turn round. Find that lost chime.

Then I went back, ears pricked to pick up the slightest sound, and as soon as I heard the sound again I made a chalk mark across the street. Stop. Turn round. Lose the found chime.

So I went back again, trying to lose the sound. Finally, having lost it, I turned, retraced my steps and went forward ever so slowly, straining my ears to catch the sound again. When I caught the first sound of the sound, I made a chalk mark across the street.

And the first chalk mark and the second chalk mark never coincided. And the third and the fourth and the fifth and the twenty-fifth never met in one place. So I would play this self-invented game. *Where does the sound begin?*

In a deserted street I, a five or six-year-old, no more, walking backwards and forwards, head cocked, listening. Walking backwards and forwards, stopping, turning round, stopping, turning round again and then marking a line in white chalk across the street. Mark the line where the sound began and ended. The one precise spot where you could hear it and not hear it. At the same time.

Hot, always hot. Still, quiet streets. Slow movements. All like a dream, a midsummer day's dream, played in the slow, eerie tempo of a summer night's nightmare; played in thick colour, greys, browns, faded red brick, blue sky, drops of yellow-white perspiration, cream curtains, cobbled black, guttered percha, chalky white.

The street criss-crossed with a tremble of white lines. No two sounds ever meeting at the same place. Heat curtaining all with heaviness and lethargy. And no lines of chalk falling together.

Backwards, forwards. Where did the sound end? Where did it begin? In my tiny mind reason demanded that the sound should, *must* end at a fixed point and start again at that same point.

It was a fantastic, frightening game for a five-year-old to play. It was a terrible game, a neurotic game. It was the limpid, untrammelled reasoning of a child proved wrong; proved to him, himself, then and there, on that breathless, airless East End street in summer time, that he was wrong. That there was no fixed point. And the immature mind refusing to accept fact. There *had* to be an answer.

So in a slow daze of lengthening time I went up and down the sad street and drew white chalk lines across it and raised my head and lifted my ears and listened for a sound of bells chiming.

And as the yawning day threw its evening cloak across the tired street and the light grew mauve-like and the white chalk began to look like a skeleton's bones, its drawn line like a line of blood, I'd give up and go home. Night and the shadows falling over a scrabble of chalk lines.

My Booba would touch my forehead, find it hot and wet, and she'd purse her lips and say to herself, in Yiddish: *Ts-ts-ts, the child is not well again*, and put me to bed. And all night long I'd dream fevered, delirious dreams of long, long roads stretching way, way out, along which I walked towards an invisible sound, an intangible view, and where I never got anywhere because, all through my dream, I kept on going back as slowly as I went forward. The dreams were funereal marches made to the muffled drumming of bells chiming.

The real crux of the tale is that no one else ever heard the bells ring. People heard a clock strike the hours. People heard the church bells chime on Sundays. But no one, no one in the whole of my world ever heard the bells I heard, chiming, chiming, chiming all day long through slow, hot summer afternoons.

I was also about five when we bought a piano. An old upright it was. I used to sit at its yellow and black keys and touch them and listen to the sound and then the echoes as they rolled away, one upon the other.

I played the game of making notes meet. One quick touch

at a note and, before it died away, another quick touch, so that the newborn note met the dying one; and then strike a third and a fourth, and listen in wonder to the mystery of blend, the magic of notes of music wrapped within other notes, the strange sound of harmony and reverberation, echo mating with echo, sound with sound, note with note, note with echo in a permutation of pianissimo.

I had names for the notes. Coloured names. This one was a blue note and that a violet. This, an orange and that a green. And I mixed the colours as I mixed the notes, till I knew exactly what sort of sound mauve and yellow and pink and green sounded like when played all together. The piano my palette and music my colours.

For hours on long winter evenings I'd sit and play the piano and talk to myself in poetry, not in prose. I'd sit there and rhyme words to make them fit the music, and I'd sit and touch the keys, delicately, never loudly, and make up words to the music and say them in time to my playing.

I wasn't taught to play. I never succeeded in playing anything known to the world as music. But I am sure I played wondrous, marvellous things, melodies unheard of, and chords unknown, and that I fashioned from the faded yellow and black notes a world of mystery no adult has ever been able to penetrate.

No one bothered me. I played very quietly. I wasn't trying to make noise. I was trying to catch colour and give it words. Just as the game with the chalk lines had been frightening, so this one was beautiful.

There I'd sit, wrapt in wonder, tinkling, stroking the keys, lost in a world I alone knew existed; and there I'd sit for hours and hours until gently moved away. And after the playing my dreams would be sweet and full of fairy music and I'd sleep like the babe I was.

My quietest hours of magic were spent at the old piano. And when they came to take it away—nobody else played it and mother could not keep up the payments, not just for *me*—I cried and cried.

I never played the piano again. Not any piano. Not any time. Never.

And I grew out of making chalk lines across the streets because the chimes of my bells began to fade.

And I grew to be seven and eight and nine and there were other things to think about. Nice things, not like chalk lines or pianos, but like Miss Rose at school and her legs. When I fell in love with Miss Rose I forgot chalk lines and pianos. When I was a five-year-old I thought as a five-year-old, but when I grew to be nine I threw away childish thoughts and started to dream exciting dreams like Miss Rose putting me across her strong thighs and spanking me on my bare behind.

Beauty faded out of my life and sex came long before its time.

Only now, many years later, do I find my heart crying for all the magic and mystery and enchantment sealed in that old piano with its faded keys, and only now do I begin again to wonder *at what point, precisely, does a sound finish and can it be picked up again, precisely, at that point?*

2　*Boyhood in the Buildings*

IN THE playgrounds of Broughton Buildings the world was miniatured. We all played together: Polacks (the children of foreign Jews), Choots (the children of English born Jews), Gentiles, coloureds, boys and girls, the children of bookmakers, prostitutes, stallholders, auctioneers, gamblers, thieves, rabbis, shopkeepers, boxers, barmen, touts, tallymen, washerwomen, chorus girls, furriers, tailors, pressers, pimps, ponces, and unemployed.

But when trouble began divisional unity took shape: Polacks versus Choots, one school versus another, one playground versus another. And trouble began easily. A disputed goal, a torn comic, a lost ball, a burst balloon—and we were at war.

Fighting would break out. But it was never vicious until the adults interfered. The Choots were all members of the same clan, all dimly related one to another. So when a Choot kid cried for his nearest relative some fourth cousin on his aunt's side would take up his quarrel; and down from the tenements would pour a horde of women to join forces with the little battle and turn it into a major war.

Aunt Aggy was the terror of all but the Choots. She was their champion. She lived right over the archway itself, so that she could look down on the playground. Cries reached her quickly. Down she would come, a tall gaunt woman to settle all strife by adding to it. She had quite the foulest mouth it has ever been my delight to hear. She could lord-mayor like a talking dictionary of profanity. She took over the centre of the stage and the Choots rallied round her while everyone else ran. She swore. She gestured. She shook. She ranted.

Her bark, I see now, was worse than her bite. She never really harmed anyone. She didn't have to. Her strident voice, screaming its foul vituperation, scared the living daylights out of child and adult alike. Even my mother moved away from Aunt Aggy—and there were very few people my mother couldn't subdue just by her mere presence.

In those days I played with a boy called Sammy—a big boy for his eight years, with a big cockeye that strabismused an otherwise pleasant face—and his sister Wendy. They were the Tuppness Twins. The kids called them "Heads" and "Tails". Sammy was "Heads". They also had a much younger twin brother and sister, then only just born. The Tuppnesses obviously didn't do things by halves. Maybe it was for this reason that the Buildings called Mr. Tuppness "Old Fourpenny".

Sammy and Wendy Tuppness were the twin children of a bookmaker and a nurse. Wendy was very fair, pretty, talkative, slim, a Choot and a tomboy; a Dresden doll about to flower into honeyed attractiveness.

Even at that undeveloped age I found myself drawn towards the opposite sex. I don't know why, but I must have been born with an overdeveloped heterosexual tendency. Girls appealed to me. Purely, mind. I had no thoughts then of sexuality or desire. I just liked the company of little girls.

I was cunning enough, even then, to stay friends with Sammy Cockeye because it meant that I could share the companionship of his twin sister. There were many hurdles to surmount in this friendship. The Choots children did not go to Hebrew classes: their evenings were free. They went to synagogue only once or twice a year, possibly on Yom Kippur, the Day of Atonement, and maybe on Rosh Hashana, the New Year. They ate *traife*, unkosher food like pork, bacon, meat—bought from English butchers—that had not had all the blood drained from it; and their parents did not salt it and prepare it in the kosher way so that not a drop of blood, not a trace, remained in the meat. They ate jellied eels which are *traife* because they swim around in the mud and are therefore unclean. They ate butter, or margarine more likely, with their meat—and no religious Jew mixes milk dishes with meat dishes.

The funny thing was that on the Passover, when religious Jews eat *matzos*, unleavened bread; use a different set of dishes and a once-a-year set of knives, forks, spoons; clean their habitations and prepare different varieties of food; wear their newest clothes; switch their eating habits and their pattern of living to remind themselves of the exodus from Egypt (hence the unleavened bread: the Israelites, fleeing from Pharaoh had to remove the bread from their oven before it had had time to rise) and the forty years of wandering in the wilderness . . . the funny thing was that on Passover the Choots did not eat jellied eels. Then they were *chometz*. In the old days bread, cake baked with flour, chocolates, sweets were *chometz*. So was everything—milk, butter, cheese and many kinds of food—that had not been prepared by new or specially cleaned machinery. Permitted foods carried a seal in Hebrew which read: *Kosher for Passover* and only foods carrying this seal were allowed to be eaten. *Chometz* and *traife* do not mean the same thing. The former applies only to foods that are not eaten on the Passover; the latter to foods that are never eaten at any time. When the Choots gave up their forbidden jellied eels on Passover because they were *chometz* they were being very funny. It was the kind of " in " joke that Polacks laughed over heartily.

The Choots rapidly became cockneyfied. They spoke in the broad vowel sounds of the true East Ender. Like them, they were brash and warm and vulgar and extrovert and funny and stout hearted and loyal to their friends and though they did not wear their hearts on their sleeves as openly as the Polacks, they could be sympathetic and compassionate . . . in an English sort of way.

The Polacks—most of whom hated the word because they hated the Poles who had never, in centuries of living close to Jews, treated them as human beings—spoke English with an accent; even the first generation Polacks accented their English with Yiddish: Polacks spoke Yiddish and their children were bilingual. Choots generally knew no Yiddish—in fifty, a hundred or a hundred and fifty years of living here they had forgotten Yiddish. They, the Choots, were so called because they hailed from Holland and Dutch is full of gutteral sounds like the " ch " in Choot.

Polacks were sadder, more serious, more religious than their Choot neighbours. They were more introverted. Their children, reared in a traditional scholarly environment seemed to do better at school; it was from Polack ranks that most of the musicians, doctors and lawyers came. Choots became bookmakers and grew rich.

Sammy, although he was a Choot, regarded me, a Polack, as a pal. We went into partnership on Passover and cut holes in cardboard shoe boxes, numbered the holes, and invited our friends to roll their Spanish nuts on to the lid of the box. If the nut went into the 2 hole we paid out 2 nuts for the one rolled, if into the 6 hole then 6. But most nuts landed up outside the cardboard lid and profits were good. We had bent the lid convexly to ensure that nuts rolled away from, not towards the holes.

On Passover we played different games from those we played all the year round. Nuts were plentiful and in season. So rolling nuts into the ring, playing cards and dice for nuts, and our nut boxes were one seasonal form of games. Passover days were holidays from school. And somehow those April hours were softer and warmer and sweeter than today's. Does distance lend enchantment even to weather?

There was a long summer of sunshine, I remember, when the sun rose like fire day after day and stayed burning bright for months on end. There were those gentle April days when we spent Passover out of doors, often taking a picnic of hard boiled eggs and *matzos* to Springfield Park, in Clapton, where there was a yearly Easter Fair. We'd tram there, swaying the six or seven miles to the Park, Sammy, Wendy and I, and spend laughing days at the fair by the banks of the River Lee; then we'd wander through the park itself, watching the cricket, bowls, tennis; have our picnic—and food never tasted so glorious—and walk and stroll some more. Home at last, tired, happy, filled with fun and memories that, I see now, would last us a lifetime.

Where are they now those golden days? Today's children don't seem to be able to enjoy the simple pleasures we revelled in or to find happiness in themselves and the company of friends. Artificiality rules today's roost. Canned music, canned entertainment, canned companionship. Sophistication is supreme. Instead of packing a small picnic parcel and going out to find where the grass is greenest and how the river runs, today's brood of immature adults demand that joy be given them, that knobs be placed to hand so that they can turn on their fun and turn it off again. Do children still walk, just for fun?

We came out of a slum and found loveliness in our living. We weren't envious of the way other children lived—who could be happier than we were, who could possibly match our moods? Eight-years-olds of this day and age are already spoilt by an advancing civilisation which has made life easier and less fun to live.

Perhaps because our flats were pokey and uncomfortably full of adults, perhaps because we had to find our own fun, perhaps because that's just the way we were, we spent our young days out of doors in the playground, in the company of other kids.

One game that had special appeal to tiny tots was to play mothers and fathers. A little boy and a little girl would stand face to face and rock their bodies at one another just as they must have seen their parents do. This performance was almost standard practice amongst the more daring. I never played it. Somehow I sensed that it was unclean, like swearing.

We'd all stand around and watch a couple performing, and laugh and laugh and none of us understood why he was laughing. We had an idea that it was some dark secret adults enjoyed, that we were not supposed to know anything about; bringing the secret out into the open was reason enough for fun. Sex meant nothing to us in those early years.

And yet . . .

In the Infants' School my teacher was a bonny Scots lass, Miss Rose. Miss Rose had short fair hair, big blue eyes, big bursting breasts and big strong legs. Short skirts were the vogue then. She wore silk stockings and high heeled shoes and showed a lot of firm leg.

We used to sit on the floor while she played the piano. And every little boy of eight or nine fought to sit near the piano so that he could look up her legs.

It was the secret we sought, not sex. What lay behind the fashionable garments? Why did adults cover up? What were they hiding? Of course it was sex, too. Freudian fumblings. But we were not aware of sex at the time though it was happening to us. Freud's children rapped a stick against railings. We did that too. But we liked looking up legs; and that's a darn sight more Freudian than rapping sticks along railings.

One day, because I was her favourite, Miss Rose bade me sit right at her legs and I had a thrilling, privileged view of muscled leg, swelling into thick shapely thighs; of stocking top, garter, white flesh and the darkness beyond where extra garments still hid the darkest secret of all from prying eyes.

I looked and looked and grew so absorbed in peering that I did not hear the silence that fell and, suddenly lifting my head, saw Miss Rose's big blue eyes staring at me. Then the class tittered. It was going-home time. She dismissed the class and pointed to me to sit where I was.

We were alone. I, on the floor, Miss Rose towering above me.

" You were looking up my skirt," she accused.

What could I say?

" Get up."

I got up.

" Then look!" she said.

And suddenly she stepped over me, pushed me under her skirt, between her legs, and began to press her thighs at me, squeezing and releasing my head in a rhythmic movement.

Her short skirt fell to my ear level. My head was in her groin. When I looked down I could see her knees and calves and the floor and light. At eye level I could just make out the white flesh of her thighs. Above my eyes it was dark and hot and dampish.

I wasn't frightened. Just bewildered. I couldn't think what she was doing, pressing and squeezing me like that between her soft thighs. She wasn't hurting me either; just a soft insistent pressure on the sides of my head, the thighs moving outwards, then closing in again to press against my ears.

The crown of my head was right between her legs and I could feel her body make a fresh movement, rocking now backwards and forwards over the top of my scalp.

Her hands were resting on the piano and her knees were gripping me tight around my waist, so that I could not duck and escape.

I remember wondering how long she would keep me prisoner like this and what the heck she was doing and wasn't this a funny way to punish somebody. There was no sense of fear at all.

And suddenly she had released me and she was staring at me, breathing a little heavily, and I was staring back at her, still ashamed of having been caught looking up her legs.

" You're not a little sneak then?" Her voice was angry.

" Me? No, Miss Rose."

" Good. You take your punishment like a man, I'm glad to see. You wouldn't want anybody to know what you were doing, would you? It was nasty, dirty, wasn't it?"

" Oh no, Miss Rose—please don't tell my mother."

" All right then. We'll both forget all about it."

" Oh yes . . ."

" Promise?"

" I promise Miss Rose."

" And you're sorry for what you did?"

" I'm sorry, Miss Rose."

And that's how the incident ended. I tried to tell my brother about it and he thought I was making it up.

All he said was " Garn!"

It wasn't for many years that I began to find Miss Rose invading my dreams. I remembered then how she loved to put the little boys over her ample thighs and pull their little trousers up skin tight and smack the soft rounded behinds with the palm of her hand. The little girls came off lightly; she used to stand them in a corner.

I remembered too that when I came out of my hiding place up Miss Rose's skirt the top of my head had been quite damp. I began to remember a lot of things about Miss Rose and by the time I was twelve I was dreaming of her constantly in ecstatic night-tortured dreams. And still I was not yet adolescent nor knew what sex was or cared overmuch. The dreaming came before the doing.

Yet, at the tender age of nine I was looking up female skirts and getting some arcane delight in the peeping, some recondite joy in the remembering. Sex was spontaneous. It arose unbidden, unrecognised.

I can't explain why I was so oversexed at that age. Was it that I was burdened with a too imaginative nature? Or that I bore deep inside me some inherited emotion that I, in my short span of living, could not have developed or brought into being on my own?

In fact I began after the incident of the legs to write poems

to Miss Rose and to post them in the school letter box, un-
signed. Only later did I realise that she must have known at
once who was writing them. At that age one's scrawl may be
indecipherable but one's fist is easily read. She never mentioned the affair or my poems. And of all the boys in the class
I was the only one she never chastised. And I longed to be
put across her thighs and smacked. I wanted to be chastised
madly.

Make what you will of it. Now I know that that was my
first and only experience with a nymphomaniac. Possibly a
very frustrated one, at that.

Poor Miss Rose. She was one of the four teachers in the
school when it received a direct hit during a midday blitz in
1941. She was then middle-aged and still unmarried and life
could not have been very kind to her. Poor Miss Rose.

But it was an isolated incident at the time in a round of
herded happenings. On Sundays, for instance, when Petticoat
Lane was crowded, the youngsters of the Building would
take their stand in the small square outside the Baths and play
diabolo to a crowd of market sightseers.

We'd throw the diabolo up high, ever so high, and catch
it unerringly. We were all pretty good at diabolo and I was
just about the highest thrower-upper of them all. I'd throw
my diabolo way, way up in the air and stand underneath it
as it came hurtling down, and catch it, and throw it up again.
We'd play throwing to one another, short fast catching, and
the crowd would applaud and throw pennies into the ring.
Sometimes, when we shared the money amongst us at the end
of the day, there'd be as much as half a crown apiece; and
that was riches indeed then.

But it was as nothing to the silver which passed hands in
the corners of the playground where the youth, the seventeen,
eighteen-year-olds and young men played cards or dice. Here
pounds were won and lost and, in the changing of money
from pocket to pocket, tempers changed too.

Sometimes the games would break up into fights. I saw
bottles broken one day and used as weapons. One tall pimply
faced boy, Harryboy they used to call him, was a devil with
the broken bottle or the cut-throat razor.

One day he was accused of cheating. Some of us younger
ones were standing at the edge of the circle and watching the

play. A short dark French boy, Oo-la-la we sometimes called him, generally Wee-wee, said he had been cheated.

Harryboy broke the lemonade bottle at his side and went for Wee-wee. Going backwards, the French boy tripped and Harryboy stuck the jagged edges of the bottle into his face and when Wee-wee got up his face was streaming blood. "Oo-la-la!" said Harryboy triumphantly. And fled.

Some months later even I, kid though I was, was surprised to see a scar-faced Wee-wee and Harryboy playing together in the same gambling school. This time they were playing dice. It happened as before, only this time Wee-wee, it seemed, had been waiting for Harryboy and kicked the bottle aside as the pimply faced young thug went for it. Then he faced Harryboy squaring up, when suddenly a razor flashed and Wee-wee went down again, blood streaming from a six-inch gash on his other cheek, the unmarked one. Again Harryboy gloated. "Oo-la-la!" he cackled. And ran.

Many weeks later I was drifting into the narrow connecting lane between the two playgrounds when I saw Harryboy being held by two sailors. Wee-wee faced him. The sailors emptied Harryboy's pockets, removed his jacket and then pushed him towards Wee-wee.

It was a terrible fight. So one-sided. Wee-wee hit Harryboy everywhere. The pimply one spat out teeth as his face was battered; sank to his knees and was yanked upright as his stomach was kicked; cried mercy as his eyes were closed. And still the battering went on. I winced and wanted to run but my legs wouldn't move. Their fight had taken them into our playground. A huge crowd formed a circle round them. And the battering went on, mercilessly.

Every time Harryboy went down, cold it seemed, the sailors yanked him upright and before his trembling knees began to give, Wee-wee would smash into him again.

The crowd watched the fight in silence. They knew that this was a revenge battle. They knew Harryboy had it coming. Finally he went down and could not be lifted into consciousness. The sailors hauled him upright then dropped him and he flopped to the asphalt like a wet sack. And then Wee-wee kicked him hard, thrice, in the ribs, and we heard them crack.

After that the Buildings never saw Wee-wee again. But

about a year later Harryboy was back in all his pimpled glory playing dice and cards and winning, always winning. But his face was badly scarred and one eye had shifted down his face where his cheekbone had been smashed.

Now and again the police would raid the playgrounds, moving in from both lanes at either side and from the front, so that there would be no escape for the gang. But the gamesters never sat down to play without posting look-outs and the shout of " Cops!" would send everyone scuttling.

These were the moments we kids waited for. We'd fall upon the money left on the floor and grab what we could and run to our flats for our lives and hide in the lavatories till things quietened down again.

The police also went for the money, coming in upon us so fast sometimes that we had to leave the kitty lying in the centre of what had been the ring and watch a hefty cop pocket the notes and the silver.

And one day, much to our glee, the police copped Harryboy. They had been hiding in one of the basement tenement doorways, silencing those who dwelt in the depths by threats; so that, when the cops appeared, they took the whole gang by surprise, cleaned up a packet of money, and nabbed them all, Harryboy included. He was out again in about a month, scars and pimples roseate-bright as ever, smiling the twisted smile only a mother could love—and then with difficulty— and spieling again.

He became a reformed character in his later years and became a voluntary collector for the Middlesex Hospital. And he died, at peace and respected, having survived the war, in an Old People's Home in Kent, in 1949.

As they grew up the youths joined the race gangs who grouped themselves in the forecourt of Aldgate East Station at the corner of Goolden Street. The most feared of these was the Aldgate Mob, a razor-slashing gang of hoodlums who protected bookmakers—for a fee—and fleeced those who would not be protected. The lucky punter coming away from the races discovered to his cost that winnings were not meant to be won permanently. They were only on loan. The race gang would take his money. Or cut him up. Or both.

In those days I accepted violence as part of the way most folks lived. But in later years I often wondered where the police were or what they were doing. They knew these gangs. They stood by and watched while, harmlessly enough I must confess, the gangsters made entrance to the station and exit from it a case of having to shove a way through vile looking villains.

Perhaps the police never caught the mobsters in the act.

But there was one day—I was about eleven then—when two gangs clashed and the razors came out and the forecourt dripped blood and still the police stood and watched. You have never seen such a mêlée. It was worse than a Twickers scrum when tempers are frayed and ears are being bitten. Bodies were intertwined in all-in wrestling poses all over the floor, razors were being wielded like floor mops, men were screaming in their agony, curses filled the air, terrified passengers huddled in corners, jackets and coats were ripped, pieces of material—and human skin—lay all over the place and the forecourt of the station ran blood. And the police watched. I saw the lobe of an ear at the toe of a copper's boot.

After about half an hour the police suddenly charged in with their truncheons, battered everyone into insensibility and carried the lot away in Black Marias. Including a few innocent bystanders.

Not many days later a few of the gangsters were back, their scars incandescent, their eyes swollen, their noses bulbously hideous, bright as prize beetroots.

In the Buildings, Abrams the bookmaker was king. If a rival appeared he never seemed to last long. Abrams was well protected, for at odd times during the day you'd see the familiar face of an Aldgate mobster by his side and watch Abrams pass money to him.

Goolden Street loved its little wager. Male and female, Jew and Gentile alike, the plain and the coloured, would sidle up to Abrams and push their crumpled pieces of paper at him and dream about coming up on a sixpenny each-way accumulator.

When the police drew near, Abrams scarpered. His lookouts gave the signal and the tubby little man would take to his legs and, looking for all the world like a bobbing beetle, would run. He'd run from one playground to another and dive deep down into one of the basement tenement entrances and hide there, if need be entering the house (a door always being kept unlocked against just such a contingency) until the all-clear was sounded. Abrams had his cover. Like the fox he was.

There were times when Abrams apparently did not pay. When irate people threatened him loudly; when only the sight of a couple of murderous looking henchmen silenced the mutterings and the oaths.

Something must have gone wrong with the protection. For Abrams was found beaten to death after a gang fight in Islington in 1954. Or maybe, being well over 70 by then, he had lost the ability to run fast away.

The Buildings' bookmakers lived a hand-to-mouth existence. When the favourites were losing the wives bought furniture and crowded the house with pianos, settees, bureaux, desks, chairs, lamps, mirrors, vases—with big pieces, the bigger the better, because they were less easy to cash in when the bad times came and the favourites started winning. The wives did not buy diamonds or jewellery or small valuable pieces or any kind of ornament which their husbands could redeem into cash. They were wise in the oscillatory pattern of bookmakers' existence. They knew the good times were followed by bad ones. They cashed in when they could. Their flats were like furniture display galleries. And the bugs made hay. There were more bugs in most of the bookmakers' flats than there are furries at the bottom of my garden.

Then suddenly everything changed.

Broughton Buildings went to the dogs.

Dog-racing came into this country and caught on faster than the hare moves. A new avenue of money-making opened up for the bookmakers. They began to coin the dough. Here, far more easily than at horse meetings, the runners could be manipulated. And were. Here there was no such thing—yet—as a clear favourite. The sport was too young for strains of breeding to have produced the class that tells. It was a great new gamble in which the punter stood less chance than he'd ever done. And the bookmakers grew stinking rich.

Abrams appeared in the playground with a fur coat, looking like a later Bud Flanagan. People began to bet on the dogs. The race gangs moved into dogland. The pickings were nearer at hand—meetings were in London—and easier.

Sammy's father, an ex-docker who had been a bookmaker's runner, set up his own book at the dogs. Sammy helped after school hours and, as soon as he was old enough to leave school at thirteen, became a full-time bookmaker's right hand man. He was a couple of years older than I was; but he still left school before his time—and Mr. Tuppness got away with it.

Sammy, who was not much of a scholar and who, normally, could not divide or multiply by more than a single figure, to whom decimals were hieroglyphics and fractions incomprehensible, was soon able to calculate odds at lightning speed, to tell you how much a bob on a 7-4 against chance going on to a 9-2, going on to a split favourite at 4-1 odds-on, amounted to.

Sammy is now one of Britain's biggest bookmakers. Yes, Sammy Cockeye, as we kids called him, is now a millionaire. And all because the Buildings went to the dogs.

But with Sammy and his father out at nights, the two younger children fast asleep, and Mrs. Tuppness bringing babies into the world, Wendy and I were often left alone in the upstairs flat. Below us lived Alice who, because she was unmarried, could use her flat as a brothel while others had to find alternative accommodation for similar pursuits. Next door lived Paddy O'Rourke with his widowed mother and two landings below lived Toby the Sweets with her two genteel daughters.

Up there, on the topmost flat of all, with the landing balcony looking high over the East End towards the river, with the Docks and Wapping and the wharves and the cranes and the gauntnesses of grey against a grey sky, Wendy and I played at love. All of a sudden, it seemed, we began to kiss and then to finger one another and in no time at all the platonic friendship of children who had grown up together became sex.

I even remember how it happened. I used to go up there when Sammy and Wendy and I were still kids at school, youngsters together, and because Mrs. Tuppness was fussy about the place being kept spotless, Mr. Tuppness and the children wore slippers which they put on as soon as they were through the front door: the front door led immediately into the front, the only living, room.

They asked me the first time to take off my shoes. I refused.

I knew my socks were full of holes and I was ashamed to take off my shoes and walk about in my socks. When they persisted, I began to lie. I told the most fantastically improbable lies. I had sensitive feet which must never be allowed to touch the floor, so the doctor had ordered. And, when they showed signs of incredulity, I was very quick with another: orthodox Jews never remove their shoes except in synagogue. This one was a real honey. Even Old Fourpenny believed it. Some of the Choots were so incredibly naïve about their own religion that you could tell them anything and get away with it.

So, that's how I began to visit the Tuppnesses, boots and all. I was about eight then and for three years or so, I was a regular two or three times a week night-visitor. I came after my own meal. I hesitate to call it dinner or supper, and sat there playing games with Sammy and Wendy until Mr. or Mrs. Tuppness came home. Usually it was Mr. Tuppness. Usually drunk but benignly so.

In all the years I was a visitor to the Tuppnesses I was never once offered a cup of tea or a sandwich. And I didn't ever think that food was due to me. In my own house my mother, even if she had had to go out, would have left behind a plateful of sandwiches and set out the cups and saucers or told my Booba to feed us. Sammy and Wendy had eaten their last meals when I arrived; and that was that, as it was in some Choot and most Gentile homes in the Buildings: the last meal was the last meal. No one ate after it. In my house we were still looking for food at midnight and one a.m. We had no hours. No set timetable. We didn't live the ordered lives our neighbours did. But at the Tuppness' house we three kids played our snakes and ladders, ludo, draughts; read our comics or books; invented dressing up games or I-spy games and were happy enough in one another's company. The thought of food never crossed our minds.

I make this point in passing. Perhaps to emphasise the meanness of the English.

I continued to visit the house when I was getting on for twelve and Sammy was going to the dogs every night. At first Wendy and I continued to try and play the same games that had kept us happy all the years. But the pleasure palled. We seemed to have grown too old for kiddish pursuits.

It all happened suddenly. One night Wendy said to me:
" What shall we play?"

I said, in a joke: " Let's play kissing."

And she kissed me. Just like that.

Suddenly we were afire. After four years of playing at
being children we began to play at being grown ups.

I kissed her, hard. She kissed me. Soon we were locked in
one another's arms.

For some weeks it just stayed at kissing.

Then, becoming bolder, my hands wandered over her
breasts. I didn't know then whether she had reached the stage
of womanhood, it was something I knew nothing about anyway, but her breasts were as big as bombs. She was quite a
slight little girl, skinny almost, but her breasts were huge and
swollen. And I began to play with them.

One thing led to another and soon I was playing with her
bare breasts and she was fingering parts of me that, until that
moment, I had never thought about as being responsive to
tactile stimuli.

Of course I knew all the talk. But I had never experienced
any real sexual excitement until then. The incident with Miss
Rose had been a subconscious inexplicable thrill. This was
consciously thrilling. We knew that, in the language of the
Buildings, we were being " dirty ".

One day we tried it. We had been working ourselves up
to a pitch and it was inevitable. She lay naked under me and
I attempted the forbidden act, the one that all the jokes were
about.

And neither of us knew how final consummation should
be achieved. We lay there, our bodies touching, but we didn't
know how to join the bodies together. I remember trying—
it is funny, now, looking back at it, but the angle of approach from the horizontal made the thing we had heard so
much about impossible.

Now I am sure that neither of us was really ready. For
there was no climax. Suddenly we both felt very tired. And
nothing had happened. We were obviously trying to make
something happen and our bodies were not ready. There was
a sign that I was ready, a visible sign; and she must have been
warmed for the occasion, for she tried to help all she knew.
But not only did we fail to make a connection; we failed to

achieve a climax. We just both grew very tired and fell asleep in one another's arms. Thus we slept for an hour or so. Then I dressed, kissed her, and went home.

The very next day I began to worry lest I had made her pregnant.

I had days, weeks and months of terror; terror which came upon me suddenly. I knew so little, really, that at twelve, getting on for thirteen, I could tell myself that there was a real fear of pregnancy when the two primary requirements for conception had not even begun to operate.

I used to look at her belly for signs of swelling. I still went up to play with her, but slowly the passion died. We had taken it to its limit, and knowing how disappointing that limit was took the edge off all the preliminaries. Slowly even the kissing died. And then we knew we didn't like one another any more and I stopped coming to the house. The friendship, the simple state of liking, of playing games together, was over.

We were not kids any more.

But neither were we grown up. We were in that in-between nether-nether land where the physical state lags some way behind the emotional one.

I was so ignorant that I knew nothing then about menstruation or I could have saved myself endless hours of panic simply by asking her the right question. But just as it is obvious to me, now, that she had not started to menstruate just as I had not yet started to make semen, what was palpably obvious at the time was that we had lain together and that a child could be born. The Bible said so. And I knew *that*.

I worked myself into such a state that I began to look ill and my Booba ts-ts-tsed over me. I think only she sensed that anything was wrong. Nobody else took the slightest notice.

Eventually, after many weeks, and after I had stopped going to her house, I met her in the street and asked her if she were pregnant.

You know what she said?

" I don't know," she said.

You can imagine what that did to me. I stopped eating, stopped sleeping, walked around in a cold sweat; yet managed to do my schoolwork well, play games and generally behave normally.

Today's kids, with all their precocious faults, are not as foolish as we were. Give two of today's thirteen-year-olds the chance and, if they're of the mind we were, there'd be neither physical nor emotional bar to consummation. And they wouldn't even need to worry about pregnancy. Not today.

It was not until the long summer holidays that I finally found my mind eased. It was about nine months after the abortive attempt at sex and I was playing in the playground when I heard a woman say something to another woman about someone having a baby.

I lost all sense of reason and went scooting up the steps to the Tuppness' flat. I don't know what I should have said if I'd got there. But, half-way up, I bumped into Wendy coming down. A new Wendy. Made up. Lips bright. Hair waved. High heeled shoes. Silk stockings. A woman now.

"Hullo," she said and swept past. I was small fry all of a sudden. She had grown up and I was still a kid, still playing kids' games in the playground. I am sure she was not consciously ashamed of having done what she did; nor even that she could not find it in her to talk to me. She had merely outgrown me; had cast me aside as one casts aside childish things.

I ran past her, noticing the slenderness of her waist and stomach, and rested on the next landing. A tremendous sense of relief swept over me. Nine terrible months of worrying went at that one moment.

It became a wonderful summer. A long, slow summer full of sunshine. We played cricket. We went on long walks into the City and far beyond that to Hyde Park. On the way we often met the long red-haired man who always carried an umbrella and walked from Mile End to Hyde Park and back twice a day and had been doing it for years. About ten miles there and back; about forty and more miles a day. Wind or sun, rain or fine, come lightning, come storm, he walked. Always carrying his umbrella.

There were many stories about him. That he had been disappointed in love and was walking it off. That he'd had a serious illness and had been told to walk. That he was looking for someone.

Yesterday, many many years later, I saw him again. Still with his long red hair streaming. Long hair, fashionable now.

Still carrying an umbrella. Still looking like a Red Indian
chief, face a little more lined, a little more weather-beaten,
but sturdily upright still, his light eyes burning in that tanned
face, his legs moving in that regular stride. Still he walked,
eyes ahead, looking neither to left nor right. A man, now
around seventy I should think, with nothing to do, except
walk.

He has been walking backwards from the East End to the
West End for the best part of his life. Heedless of people,
of weather, of the world it seems, he walks. And he never
talks to a soul. When I was a kid I wanted to go up to him
and say "How?" Now, when I see him, he makes me feel
sad. He is a part of all that lostness that has gone with the
changing East End.

For the East End today is not what it was. The excitement,
the life, the colour have fled. Few Jews live there these days
—it is an area of coloureds: Jamaicans, Indians, Africans—and
these people are far more conservative in their behaviour
than we were, paradoxical though this may seem to some.
They reserve their joy for special occasions and, with the
exception of the daily market in Wentworth Street and the
Sunday one in Petticoat Lane, still largely Jewish in ambience,
weekdays in the East End now are as quiet and uneventful as
in any of the suburbs of London.

I got near to the East End again when I was in Manhattan
recently. There I felt again the life pulsating through a community; the bustle, the noise, the shops open twenty-four
hours a day; could eat food that, because it was so European,
Asiatic and Slav, was almost typical Jewish food: pickled
cucumbers, chopped liver, cheese cakes, blintzes, salt beef,
postrami, lutkas, apfel strudel, sour cream, lemon tea; could
know again the heart-warming sensation of life being fully
lived; could sense the vibrancy, the urge, the surge of existence.

In parts of Manhattan today a boy can enjoy the kind of
life I lived as a boy, with all its crowded wonder, all its lively
fullness and fun, all its sadnesses, its sensitivity, its spur to
the imagination.

The man who walks is a living symbol of an East End that
has gone. And he is probably not even aware of it. What is
he aware of?

One of the games I most enjoyed as a boy was a game I invented, or thought at the time I had invented. We divided into two lots and one group went off towards the back streets of the City, deserted on Saturday afternoons and Sundays when these games were played.

The party running away laid chalk trails, some of them false, but one always true. Every hundred paces we had to stop and mark an arrow to point the direction in which we were going. To slow up the following group, who had to count up to five hundred before they could give chase, members of the fleeing group were detailed to lay false trails and away they would go in wide circles to chalk on walls and pavements for a mile or so, every hundred paces, before meeting up with us again at an appointed place at an appointed time.

For youngsters such as us it was a highly developed sort of game. Timing had to be exact. Distances had to be calculated. If I detailed a couple of lads to set false trails I had to plan the precise time of remeeting some miles ahead. If we had to wait for them we might get caught. If they had to wait for us they risked capture. And one had to know the East End and City like one's own playground.

The City of London at week-ends when business has shut down has a dignity and secluded charm even its regular work-time inhabitants can't know. The squares lie quiet. In the alleyways the posts that Doctor Johnson compulsively touched make ideal chalking places. In the shallow areas of austere commercial houses lie hiding places where one may crouch and watch the enemy pass; where, as one of my boyhood friends and I used to do, coins can be saved behind a loose brick in an area wall.

Up we'd go, across Middlesex Street, into Harrow Alley and through a narrow road into Devonshire Square, one of the truly memorable places of my boyhood. It stood like an oasis in a wilderness of noise. Less than two hundred yards away Liverpool Street roared its head off. About half a mile away in the other direction Aldgate fanfared and trumpeted. Yet here was a ghost square where, in broad daylight on a Sunday afternoon, no pedestrian passed and the tall Edwardian and Victorian houses slept after a week's rushing and wild overcrowding.

From Devonshire Square across the traffic-bound Liverpool Street, down Broad Street and into Finsbury Circus, and back up Hounsditch and into Aldgate. Perhaps, then, across into Mansell Street and down towards the Tower. Into the grounds to sit across the old cannon, stroll by the river and wait for our trail misleaders to catch up with us. Perhaps a hasty sandwich and a drink from a lemonade bottle filled, alas, with water only; the thirsty throat gulping at the tepid liquid, the eyes watching the glass ball in the neck of the bottle bobbing up and down.

Where have all the glass balls in lemonade bottles gone?

Sammy Cockeye usually led one group. In his group his sister, Wendy, was his *aide de chasse*. Without letting my own group know what I was doing I used to go down into one of the areas of the Devonshire Square houses—the same area every time. They thought I was urinating. Each member of the group had his own favourite watering spot. Down in my own area I'd prise a loose brick out of the wall and leave love messages for Wendy. It had all been arranged between us on an unaccompanied walk we'd taken one Sunday through the City.

I knew that sooner or later the pursuing mob would invade Devonshire Square. It was the short-cut route to Liverpool Street and they knew that my group would take it. But the game was played to the rules and chalked arrows had to be followed.

Behind the loose brick lay a rectangle of darkness and loose rubble into which, as a boy of ten, I could get my arm right up to the elbow. My fingers would push the note deep down into the remotest corner.

I love you, the simplest note might say. Or, *Will you marry me?* Or, *Ralph loves Wendy*. All good clean fun. And I knew when she got the notes. She'd tell me.

Just after the war, when my own particular part of the Buildings had been laid waste and Wendy was a famous film star and I used to try to avoid having to walk down Goolden Street because the memories that came came with pangs of sentiment, I was at Liverpool Street Station and found myself with an hour to spare.

Something clicked in my brain and I felt myself being drawn towards Devonshire Square. It was a quiet September afternoon. Saturday. The square was deserted. It looked mellow and serene in the thin afternoon sunshine. I found myself walking towards the secret house of my boyhood. I went down the area steps. I found the brickwork much as it had been and the brick still loose; it did not yield as it used to to my fingernails: I had to pick at it with a nail file before it came into my hand.

My arm wouldn't go very far inside before my fingers met solid resistance. I remember thinking: it isn't deep at all— not more than a few inches, that's all.

I was groping around with my fingers when they hit a folded piece of paper. I pulled it out, opened it and there, scrawled in a hand I could not recognise as my own was the message: *Roses are red, violets are blue, Wendy Tuppness I love you. From guess who?*

I don't know how long I stood there with that scrap of paper in my hands. The years fell away and I was a boy again, in love again, unworldly, unconcupiscent, uncomplicated. Dear Wendy Tuppness. Weep for the past that's gone. Weep for myself. For childish games and boyish pranks and innocent pleasures. Cry for the lost years. Where have they gone? It was only a moment ago, a bare moment ago, that I was diving down into this area, secreting this little note, yelling to my comrades, living excitedly and being able to enjoy, in its actuality of being, the very second of time. Nostalgia gripped me. And the afternoon, suddenly tired of seeking the faint sun, turned slowly to greyish blue and then to sad purpled magenta, the colours as faded and faraway as boyhood was, the autumnal air depressing and dank and drear.

I gave myself up to a pathetic fallacy of my own making, with the fading day and the weather playing a Kreutzer Sonata accompaniment to my mood.

It seemed to me that life had slipped by. And, remembering it all now, how much more deeply is this pain felt, how much more telling the realisation. For an age in Thy sight is but as a watch in the night. We are words on the pages of life in the book of Time. The moving finger marks them for a fleeting insubstantial second and passes them by. Flash— we're here; flash—we're gone.

Wendy Tuppness would never again be a slim fair young girl with eternity in her eyes, and my boyhood was a shadow even in my own memory. How good it was to strive, to seek, to play at love. How sad it was to remember.

I climbed out of the area steps like a man who has seen the ghost of himself when young. And I began to recall the other childish pastimes that had lightened those years.

Tents. Tents we built in the playground and under which we sat for hours on end. Tents made of bits of planking, sheets of cardboard, newspapers. Tents in the brown playground on long languorous summer days. Oases in a desert of slums.

Downstairs in our own flat my brother Ben and I would build a tent in the dark back room where all the stock of the barrow was kept. In this room my Zaida slept. The room was piled with junk. It obscured the windows, shutting out the light.

In this unlit room we'd throw a blanket over two piles of junk, prop the sagginess up with one or two of the stall's corner irons, move some cushions into the tent, spread ourselves out and while away long magical hours in talking.

Ben was two years older than I and I looked up to him as my protector. And when he began to tell me about soldiers that moved, walked and marched when you wound them up, about a boy who had promised to get them for us if we paid him two shillings per soldier, I found myself looking straight into fairyland.

We both played with toy soldiers. And our dream had always been to possess ones that moved; soldiers marching, cavalry galloping, Red Indians creeping and cowboys whirling their wild lassoos. The idea took hold of us and we began to daydream until, in the darkness of tent time, fancy and reality were all mixed up.

And we'd sit in the tent and talk for hours about moving toy soldiers. The games we would have. The battles we would win.

Sitting in the tent there, in darkness, my face turned eagerly towards my brother and he, Ben, talking about the dream coming true and I seeing it all. He believed it as much as I did; and I certainly believed everything he believed in then.

Ten-years-old. Ten marvellous years old. Toy soldiers that walked and ran and fell down and were killed and never died.

In the darkness. Dreaming. O, such beautiful dreams, such simple dreams. Dreams of wonder. Limpid dreams deep with magic.

We saved our halfpennies and met the boy, a big ape-like boy, and gave him our savings. Every Sunday we'd meet him at the far end of Petticoat Lane where the tail end of the market gave us room to stand three abreast on a pavement. We passed over our halfpennies and the big boy wrote figures in a book and we went away happy and still dreaming.

This went on for weeks. Ben and I would save every half-penny we could scrounge—it amounted to about sixpence or so a week: a lot of money to us in those days—and give it to the boy every Sunday.

Occasionally Ben would tell him that we had paid him more than two shillings and were entitled to at least one soldier. We also kept a reckoning. But with some excuse or other we were fobbed off. I remember the best excuse: that they could only be purchased in boxes of twelve and we had to keep on saving until we had saved twenty-four shillings.

He was the first gangster and we were the first suckers. How gullible is youth! How credulous! Ours was a simple faith. We wanted to believe. And the big boy was shrewd enough to be able to feed our imagination with improbable tales we longed to hear.

And then, one day, he wasn't there. And Ben discovered he had left the neighbourhood. And finally an adult laughed at us and our dreams were shattered.

We used to sit in the dark tent and dream and give voice to our dreams. It was a little secret we shared. A dream we halved. Those were days full of mystery, wild with imagin-ings. And when the dream was shattered we never built a tent in the back room again.

3   *Kleine Menschen*

MY ZAIDA was very curious about "the dogs". Everybody in the Buildings was going to the dogs. He'd heard the word and he could not understand what it meant.

"*Hinnt?*" he would say to us. "*Vie geht minn tsoo a hinnt?* A dog? How does one go to a dog?"

We explained that the dogs chased a hare, forgot to mention that the hare was a false one, and sowed the seeds for one of the funniest episodes of my days in the Buildings.

For eventually my brothers and I decided to take Zaida to the dogs. We took the tram to Clapton and went through the turnstiles, Zaida eyeing the metal fingers round his waist with consternation, and down to the rails.

The first race was signalled. The hare flashed by, the traps were opened, and the dogs flew.

We were about a hundred yards to the left of the winning post. The dogs flashed past us the first time so quickly that Zaida barely had time to understand what was happening. But when the hare zipped past him the second time it was plain he *had* understood. For before any of us could stop him he had climbed the wire fence, agile as ever, had run into the centre of the track and was waving his arms and yelling as the dogs came pelting towards him, the favourite leading by many lengths.

He managed to stop the favourite even though the other dogs eluded his grasp. There was a roar from the crowd, consternation everywhere, and the race was declared void. Pandemonium raged. Zaida was taken into custody.

We followed Zaida sadly to the local police station. They put him into the cells for the night. We didn't know what to do. We dare not tell mother—she would go crazy with shame and worry, mostly, we felt, with shame. Her father in prison! It couldn't happen.

But as we left the station a man approached us and asked us what had occurred. He was a big man, a fierce-looking man, so we told him. He told us to hang on. We waited. Within the hour he was back with a fussy little fellow, a solicitor as it turned out. We all went into the station and after a great deal of argy-bargy Zaida was freed.

The bookmakers, many of whom knew Zaida and respected him, were celebrating the defeat of a favourite by acknowledging that Zaida was responsible for that defeat. They had paid his bail.

Next morning, without telling mother, we whisked Zaida away and went to court.

An interpreter was provided for Zaida. It was explained that Zaida wished to protect the poor little hare from the dogs. Asked if he had anything further to say my Zaida trotted out his three pet phrases. All together. He was obviously conscious that the occasion merited the conjoint use of the sonorous rejoinders he was in the habit of uttering, one at a time, when roused.

These gems of repartee were: " I got vitnesses for . . ." (with a resounding swear word attached); " I got bankers for . . ." (with another good word added); and " I got miny-uns for . . ." (plus a sacred word). The last, construed by the erudite as *minions* and by the rank and file as *millions,* was of course neither. A *minyun* is a gathering of ten male adults necessary before prayers can be said; but either way, it more or less conveyed the meaning Zaida wished to make clear. If he had living affidavits to his deeds he was happy. The action was justified. The sightseers could bear vitness to it.

In court, asked to speak, and expected to talk in Yiddish so that the interpreter could translate his words to the magistrate, he suddenly said, in his booming voice,

" I got vitnesses de dogs runs noch dus haircatz and I got bankers dey go to catchumalive and I got a minyun dey goes meshugah. Venn I stop front hinnt der mans says to me I am old bleeding bastard. I got vitnesses for old and I got bankers for bleeding and I got a minyun for bastard!" The last part of his defence was a joy of histrionics. He waved his arms and thundered the words to a horrified court.

The magistrate permitted himself a wry smile.

" Case dismissed," he said.

Outside, we were surrounded by a horde of grinning, laughing, friendly bookmakers. They pressed pound notes into Zaida's hands. We counted them. There were thirty-five in all.

He came home proudly and, as always when he made some money, pressed the notes into my mother's hands and said: " Nah."

How can one translate " nah "? It is being ten feet tall when giving. It is saying, " Look, I give you this like a king distributing largesse." It is a hundred words, a hundred moods in one.

There's another word like it in Yiddish: *noo? Noo* is always a question mark. It says what-are-you-doing? and when-are-you-doing? and where-are-you-going? and why-are-you-going? and, mostly, what-about-it?

It reminds me of the story of the Jewish son who came into his father's business full of bounce, brashness and bold, modern methods. Like a lot of good Jews the boy was an accountant, qualified. Whoever heard of trying to make a living, unqualified?

So he looks at the books and discovers that Moishe across the road is owing his father five hundred pounds and, what's worse, that he has been owing such a sum for a long time. This is terrible.

" Father," he storms, " is this a way to run a business? That a friend should owe you so much money and you do nothing about it. How do you expect we are ever going to make a profit? Father you must let me write him a note, a strong note."

" Do what you think fit, mine son," said the father.

So the son wrote a note, a strong one and waited for the reply. And waited. And grew fed up waiting and wrote another. Still no reply. Angered, he wrote a third, a blistering note, threatening the law, gaol, incarceration, bankruptcy, torture, disgrace. But no reply was forthcoming.

In desperation he went to his father and said he would have to sue Moishe.

" Sue-shmue," said his father and scribbled a note and folded it and sent it across the road with the tea boy.

Less than ten minutes later back came the money wrapped in another sheet of paper. The full five hundred pounds.

The son was amazed.

"What did you write, father? And what did he reply?"
Father handed son both notes.

Father had written: *Noo?*

Moishe had written: *Nah.*

So Zaida put the money into his daughter's hands and said
Nah. Here you are. Here it is. See what I bring you.

He didn't work. Synagogue took up too much of his time.
Going to *shool* every morning, afternoon and evening meant
mother being left to superintend the barrow.

Sometimes he took his time about coming back from *shool*,
too. The old fellows of the congregation, those who formed
a regular *minyun* at the synagogue and without whom prayers
would not have been possible, for it was their presence that
constituted a quorum—these old men would repair to the
urinal in Wentworth Street, part of the daily market known
as Petticoat Lane on Sundays, and stay there talking, philosophising and putting the world to rights.

It was known to my Zaida as *Die Pish-hooskie.* The last
part of the word means little house; the remainder should be
self explanatory. There they'd foregather and discuss learn-
edly abstruse questions of religion or, just as knowledgeably,
the burning topic of the day. They were great fun to listen
to, for they had only an elementary idea of what went on
about them, picking up crumbs from half-heard conversations or the Yiddish newspapers; and these, to say the least,
weren't exactly oracles of information.

For instance my Zaida would say something like: "Ramsay MacDonald is going to build a new synagogue in Wentworth Street, just where this urinal stands" (all in Yiddish,
of course); and one of the wiseacres would reply with: "He
won't do it. This urinal was opened by King George and if
Ramsay MacDonald tries to interfere with it, King George
will send him to the same island where Napoleon went—Long
Island in New York." Then someone would say something
like "Long Island is in Chicago, my daughter lives there," and
they'd be away.

The conversations were just as inaccurately mirth-provok-
ing as this.

My brother, Mark, who was an excellent mimic, used to
go down into the urinal and listen in to their philosophising

and come home creased with laughter to regale us with hilarious renderings of the conversations and discussions he had heard.

Zaida was not, you will appreciate, one of the world's workers. But at certain times of the year, Passover for instance, he was in great demand. Firms making cakes and biscuits for Jewish consumption had to clean their machinery and use only certain prescribed products. The Kosher seal could only be put on those provisions that had earned it from the *Beth Din*, the House of Law. The Beth Din therefore employed watchers who sat by the machines and watched them and came home, as Zaida did every Passover, laden to the eyebrows with cakes and biscuits, and with money paid by the authorities.

One particular Passover Zaida was watching the machinery at quite a big factory. What he was watching he probably did not know. Ingredients went in, the machines went round and Zaida sat and snoozed.

Someone told him that day to call when the needle on a dial went up to a certain mark. And Zaida nodded and promptly went off to sleep and was awakened by the sound of fire engines and found himself surrounded by smoke, and men in uniform all round him.

That year the Passover products of this particular factory were in very short supply. Zaida, like Alfred, had burnt the cakes.

Passover was a great day in the house. Friends from far and wide were invited and we sat down, twenty, thirty or more to a chain of tables put together to form one great festive board, covered with the whitest of cloths, laden with wines and *matzos* and food and fruit; and we prayed a little and ate a lot.

There were the immediate members of the family including such as Uncle Lotting, the dapper Savile Row tailor. And friends like Morry Leshy, Cockeye Sam, John Mather, Itzik Foortzer, Solly Shumer, Manny Field, Dr. Deacon, Roger Bageot, and a host of people who were close friends of my brothers and sisters. There were seven of us and each invited at least one close friend.

The ceremony begins with a reading of the *Hagadah* which tells the story of the Exodus from Egypt. The youngest—

that meant me—read the Four Questions, the first of which
begins " Why is this night different from all other nights?"
and goes on to ask " Why do we eat unleavened bread? . . .
Why do we rinse the hands?" and " Why do we lean?" The
Hagadah answers all the questions. At length. Then, after
three large glasses of wine taken during the course of the
reading, the meal is served. After the meal another large glass
of wine, strictly Palestinian and Kosher, is drunk. Four in all.

The first of the Four Questions reminds me of the tale of
the very orthodox Jew who had done great work for the
community and was awarded a knighthood. It was the eve of
Passover when he had to appear before the Queen to receive
the accolade. All knelt. When the Queen came to the holy
man she noticed that he had neither knelt nor removed his
hat. And she said: " Why is this knight different from all
other knights?"

The serving of the Passover meal kept my Booba going
all day. Mother helped a little; but Booba did most of the
work—making the chopped liver, the *charoseth*—sweet herbs
pulped in wine, frying the fish as no one has ever been able
to fry fish, preparing the chicken, raisining the apfel strudel.
It was the meal of the year. I wonder now, but only now,
how we found the money to pay for it.

Then the singing. The old traditional tunes reaching high
up into the street and playground outside, where crowds of
Choots assembled just to hear us sing. My brother Ben had
a fine voice. My brother-in-law Alf had won competitions
for singing. Uncle Adolf had a rich resounding baritone. And
how they sang. *One pet kid—chad gadyoh;* and the catchy
bimhayroh song which could easily go into the top pops today.

Finally, the last note. The note they all held on to to try
and emerge as winner; and when they were all bursting for
breath my Zaida's voice, still holding the note, still supreme.
And they'd give way, graciously, and let Zaida finish it in
his booming bass.

Then we'd walk Uncle Lotting home and he'd recite
Shakespeare to the stars, sing arias from his favourite operas,
and say to every passing policeman, " Constable—what a
lovely moon!"

And Zaida, who had also looked upon the wine when it

was red, would take a stroll round the playground, a slow measured stroll and then retire to his back room.

And the guests would stay on till three or four in the morning, chatting, telling jokes. Booba would make innumerable cups of tea and the night would pass until on the East End street the bald day broke.

Such nights. Such togetherness. They don't make Passovers like that any more.

My Booba used to say we celebrated it because we wanted not the *Hagadah* but the *ulkas*, not the prayers but the delicious flour balls rolled in chicken fat that go into the soup.

Booba. There's sadness in remembering her. For she worked all the days of her life. She never saw the sea. Never saw the country. Never went out, except to a few shops around the corner. She was always old. I knew her about twenty-five years in all and she never changed. She was old when I was at my first stage of recall and she was the same, wrinkled and lined and stooped, when she died.

She lived for her grandchildren. The boys especially. They were her favourites. In descending order: the eldest, Alf, first; then Mark, Ben, and me. But she loved us all. She grumbled and she complained, but there was nothing she would not do for us.

I try hard to imagine her as a child and I can't. Did she never play childish games, twirl a skipping rope, weave garlands of flowers for her hair, run merrily from the boys? Was she ever young? All her life she was old and all her life she worked; and there is sadness to remember her lined face and her thin, frail body and how she so seldom laughed.

Zaida had a sense of fun, reflected in his twinkling eyes; but Booba never laughed.

She bore everything stoically: illness, the death of loved ones—her son-in-law, my father, and two brothers I should have had who died before I was born—her uprooting from her native Russian fields to tenement and slum, her inability to understand what people round her were saying.

She wore the *shaitel*, the wig orthodox women put on when they were married; and she went to synagogue on the Holy Days. The rest of the time she stood downstairs in the basement front room and cooked and washed and scrubbed and waited for her grandchildren to come home.

She died of tiredness in her late seventies. She was worn out, that's all. Her tremendous capacity for work gave out and she went to her bed reluctantly and passed away as quietly, as simply as she had lived.

She died in bed, surrounded by love. She was lucky, I suppose. She had left her mark on life. Out of one daughter she had amassed seven grandchildren and four great-grandchildren. The world would forget her, but we wouldn't. We did not light the *yahrzeit* light (kindled every year on the anniversary of a loved one's death) for her for more than a few years. We did not say *Kuddish* (the prayer for the dead) for her for very long. But we remembered. We always remembered. We missed her more when she was gone than when we had taken her for granted, deluding ourselves that her work for us was something we could take in perpetuity.

We missed her a lot.

But perhaps she was fortune-favoured after all, despite all the work and the hardship and the ignorance of pleasure, as we know it, and the absence of tangible reward.

For she had her immortality. She did not live to see millions of us go into the gas chambers; it did not occur to her that, as a Jewess, she was something special, something uniquely objectionable to some.

She was never bothered with abtruse thoughts. Music meant little to her. Poetry did not exist. A few people spoke English, but enough of them spoke Yiddish to make her words understandable, the few words she ever said.

She was what she was. There were Gentiles, *goyim*, of course, but they never really entered her span of being. Religion was something she grew up with, unquestioning, the one God, one Father in Heaven to whom she prayed on the appointed days. Wasn't that what the whole world did?

She knew other countries existed. She had lived in Russia. But names like America and France were just names. Even names like Southend and Brighton were only names to her. Her world was the Buildings and it was populated by her immediate family and that was enough.

She was never to know the shame of standing naked before the grave one had dug for oneself; the horror of seeing one's own children mutilated before one's eyes; never to feel bewildered by the stories of Jewish torture; never to fear for the lives of her loved ones. Around her as she lay dying was the future, her future.

And we remember her.

We remember her wonderful way of christening people. They had unpronounceable names like Cohen or Levy or even Smith. That conveyed nothing. Names had to reveal character, had to have the same force as they must have done in her childhood when Moishe was Moishe the Butcher; and Chaim, Chaim the *Fershloffener*, the sleepy one.

There was Itzik Czenczlizk, a man whose name we could only have pronounced with a cough and a spit anyway. He played spoons in the market and he talked in Spoonerisms. I wanted to call him Itzik Spooner, but my grandmother had noticed that he often let wind and she called him Itzik Foortzer. It was the perfect name. He became Itzik Foortzer and was known from then on by that onomatopoeic appellation.

Mrs. Dickle had the herring stall in the market. We bought our cucumbers from her. She would bend over the barrel, a big woman, big buttocks thrust outward, and plunge her arm up to her elbow in the brine. Booba called her Mrs. Dickle Pickle. It was so right.

She first "yiddished" Sammy Tuppness into Sammy Cock-eye and she would have gone on calling him that even had she lived to see him make his first million. Solly Shumer who stuttered she called Solly Shtumer (the dumb one). He was also to make a million and the how of it bears telling.

I used to press my own pants once or twice a week. After I had reached the age of thirteen and had come out of short trousers the day I celebrated my Barmitzvah, it was necessary to take care of the long 'uns I wore. They were the only pair I had.

Pressing them one day I was surprised to find all six feet of Solly Shumer bending over me. He was a friend of my brother Ben and, already nearing seventeen, had been out at work in a tailor's shop for almost four years. So when he began to *kibbitz* over my pressing I asked him how he would do it.

He showed me how to take the bags out of the knees by rolling the iron towards the outer edge of the knee and suddenly he stopped short and said: " Th-th-th-that's it. A ro-ro-ro-tary i-i-i-iron."

" A what?"

He began to explain. He had just been seized with an idea. Seeing me pressing had given him an idea. Revolving irons that could be automatically operated, thus achieving uniform over-all pressing without a man behind the iron, without a fellow having to bend himself double and rupture himself pushing a ton weighted iron to the far corners of a garment he could not reach normally.

That idea took hold of Solly and from that day on he began to experiment. Within three years he had produced a prototype and within five he had his own factory. By the time war broke out Solly Shumer was managing director of a big clothes company. During the war he made uniforms. After it his first million. Solly Shtumer, with the " t ", who got his grand idea when he was watching me press my one and only pair of trousers. He stuttered. And made a million.

Today I'd have to go through six secretaries before I could even be refused an appointment by his personal assistant.

Paddy Rourke Booba " yiddished " into Paddy Footbollick and Morry Lesher into Morry Sorry. She called the local roadsweeper, whose name apparently was Alfie Moss, Mossy-ossy-shit. She was not being vulgar. Yiddish has the peculiar quality of taking words for natural functions and using them naturally. Zaida's Pish-ooskie and Mossy's ossy-four-letter-word can be uttered in the politest Yiddish speaking company. In fact, you've only to say *Ich bettach dir tzoo far-zeihen*—I beg you to overlook this—and you can then come out with a string of four letter words that would do credit to the Chatterly gamekeeper or Joyce's Bloom.

One of my sisters could have married Solly Shumer. But he didn't quite measure up to her idea of what a man should be. I remember how she heard the news that he had become a millionaire. " So what?" she said. Good for her.

Booba even had names for her own brood. Pet names I suppose they were. She called me *Vunce*—little bug, and my brother Ben, who was a chubby kid, Pom-pom.

When he was about fourteen Ben got bitten by the wireless craze. It was a new thing then. Ben began to buy little bits and pieces and to wire them together. The room in which he worked, our upstairs living-room, began to resemble a junk shop. Wire trailed everywhere. Screws littered the floor.

Bits of solder ate their silvered way into our best table top.
Odd tools found the soft end of your anatomy as you sat.
Small pieces of vulcanite scratched you as you got into
bed.

But slowly a thing took shape. It had its home in the back
room in which mother and the girls slept, and crept by stages
and condensers and coils and wire, always wire, into the next
room and round the room with more weird looking circles of
white wire and dials and knobs, to end finally in a pair of earphones.

Wire *less* indeed. Mother complained. My brothers swore.
My sisters grumbled. But Ben was bent on achievement. He
could have been Edison himself as he worked far into the
night completing his circuit.

And one day, he, bursting with excitement, called us to
him and there, in the headphones, was sound. 2LO and the
Savoy Orpheans. Music from the spheres. We fought to get
the earphones over our head and marvelled and sighed with
wonder when we did. What would they think of next? They,
indeed. What would *Ben* think of next?

He thought of it. He put the earphones into a vase and the
magnified sound went round and came out. Then we could
all listen to Carrol Gibbons.

Booba listened. She had been summoned upstairs from her
downstairs abode. It was rare for her to make the ascent. She
arrived wondering what all the fuss was about.

Lips compressed, thin hands folded, she sat down and we
grew silent so that she could listen in.

There was no answering glint of excitement in her eye.
Her demeanour didn't change. She kept her lips compressed.
Then, as we all looked at her—

"*Kleine menschen,*" she said. There was no exclamation
mark. It was a summing up.

She put her hand into the vase, rummaged around, and
pulled out the earphones. She would not have them put over
her head, so we held one tight against her ear. She listened.

"*Kleine menschen,*" she said positively.

Little people. We could not persuade her otherwise. We
tried telling her that people were sitting in a room about ten
miles away and the instruments she could see were picking up
the noise and reproducing it. Not very easy to say in Yiddish,

at least not in the simple kind of untechnical Yiddish my grandmother knew. But we said it. And all she said was "*kleine menschen.*"

Now my Zaida, perhaps because he was less naïve, more in touch with people than his wife, could accept what we were saying. But it did not excite him. He did a so-what, as if to say *Noo?*—what's-all-the-fuss-about? and left us sitting there gaping. In the years that followed, when radio became a standard component of any home, Zaida never once took time off to listen to it. It meant nothing to him.

He took the changing world in its stride. Cars for broughams, broughams for carts, carts for walking—it was all one to him. And he had seen a lot of changes in his lifetime. He had seen gas being first used to light houses. Then electricity. He had seen the steam engine come. Bicycles. Cars. He had seen the early phonograph, the record player, the gramophone. Now he was hearing radio. So what? He didn't live to see television, but he had once been taken to the cinema and that meant nothing to him. TV would have left him unmoved too.

He was interested in *people*. He loved animals. Life entertained him—he could mimic the local milkman, postman, policeman, bookie with a Yiddish-English impersonation that was excruciatingly funny because, though it was so bad, was still recognisable as a caricaturish impersonation of someone we knew.

But *things* left him cold. Inventions, architecture, flowers, clothes, material comforts—these meant less than nothing to him. He didn't understand machinery and he didn't want to understand it. If it made noises, it made noises. Big deal.

My Booba, on the other hand, liked her gas stove. It was so much easier than the old cooking stoves she had used way back in the homeland. She cheered with the rest of us when the Buildings went over from gas lighting to electricity. She liked the chain in the loo and the way the water did the job she was quite prepared to tackle not only for herself but for every member of the family.

She had no idea how or why things worked. But they saved time and they were good. She did react while her husband couldn't have cared less.

But for some reason she refused to accept the miles of

wires we called wireless that linked up into a single instrument from which noises emerged.

It was little people. And, had we not prevented her, she would have torn the earphones apart to prove her point. Ben forestalled her by unscrewing the flat earpiece and showing her the magnets and the coils inside.

"*Kleine menschen*," she said and prodded with her finger towards the bowels of the apparatus.

We did not have a telephone. But Alice in the next block did. Alice needed it: it was essential equipment for her work. So we persuaded Alice to allow Booba to be at the phone while my eldest brother rang her up. He was her favourite and she would know his voice.

It was all duly arranged for a Sunday morning and the phone rang and we heard my brother's voice and we pushed Booba into position and put the hand instrument into place against her ear. We heard him say, "Hullo, Booba—*vos machst doo?* How are you?"

This time she stiffened. She threw the phone down.

This time, she protested, the little people had gone too far. They were imitating her grandchild's voice.

Half an hour later my brother was trying furiously to persuade her that he had indeed talked to her. She just shook her head and closed her ears and refused to believe. Zaida, on the other hand, had been brought to a telephone in a factory he was guarding one Passover. Someone in authority was asking questions. Zaida, we were told, answered the phone as though he had been born with one at his side; he never queried that he had been spoken to, nor that when he had spoken someone had heard what he said; it was the first time he had ever used the instrument and it left him with absolutely no reactions one way or t'other.

My Zaida knew it wasn't really people who made things work. It was God. God made the trams runs on lines, the trains on rails, the cars move along the streets. God made the telephone talk and the wireless play. People only thought they did it.

Booba never believed it was God. For her it was some kind of inexplicable magic and the less she thought about it, the better. She, for example, believed fervently in a Dybbuk, a wicked spirit that could enter a human body and drive it mad. She had seen Dybbuks exorcised and cures effected. She *knew* this to be true. People did not go mad. They were invaded. Wireless and the telephone had some connection with Dybbukry. She wasn't prepared to think about it.

She never really thought deeply about anything. She was a simple soul, almost a child in her attitude towards life. But she accepted an adult responsibility from a very early age: she was married at sixteen and my mother was born before she was seventeen. She had one other child, also a daughter, but it died at birth.

There is not a lot to write about Booba. Her life seemed to be uncomplicated. And hard. She wasn't easy to know or easy to like. But we, her grandchildren, loved her with an abiding love because, I think, we sensed the devotion she had for us. We were her life. She worked for us. She slaved for us. She lived for us. She adored us far more than she adored my mother, her only child. Mother was much too clever for her. They spoke a different language of living. But we, the grandchildren, made the effort to meet Booba at her stage of understanding; we grew up with her and we retained our childlike dependence on her.

Booba grumbled a lot—about our habits, our untidiness, our anger, even our laughter. She hated people who laughed too easily and, uncannily, she seemed to be intuitively correct in the violent dislike she took to some people who were always laughing. She was right in her assessment. They all turned out to be bad eggs. She grumbled a lot. But she never grumbled about her own disappointments. She never complained. She never murmured that work was too hard, the hours too long, that she did not feel well, or suggested that she needed something, anything. Even her grumbling was selfless.

Booba and her *kleiner menschen*. Dear, dear Booba.

The *kleiner menschen* made big trouble for Ben. He began to get orders from people in the Buildings for sets. He began to build one for the bookmaker who employed Abrams as a second string. This big man's name was Charlie Grose and he was a big man and so Booba called him Charlie der Grosser (the Big One). Right on the head, as usual.

He commissioned Ben to build him one of the new fangled radio sets complete with curved horn loudspeaker—the latest in gadgetry.

Ben set about his task with unusual alacrity. The promise of big money from the big man was just around the corner. Charlie der Grosser was known to be the kind of man who was big in everything; if things went well his rewards were big too. Ben worked and hoped.

My brother's particular chum at the time was a boy called Laurie Lachman. He was a tall, roly-poly sort of a lad, with a mass of curly black hair he could never keep in order. It fell all over his round, fleshy face. He wore steel spectacles tied together, where they had been broken many times, with bits of tape and string. He had little pig eyes. And Booba disliked him because he always laughed. He never stopped laughing.

Now people like my brother-in-law Dave laughed too; but only at jokes, never all the time. Laurie laughed ceaselessly. A cackling, throaty laugh it was, the unmusical chortle rumbling around that swollen throat like sounds blown into a French horn.

My Booba's name for this schizophrenic was *Lacher* which means, literally, Laugher. Obvious, when you come to think of it; but we didn't—Booba did.

Lacher had been reading all about radio and he knew just about everything there was to know about it. And then some. He stood at Ben's elbow while Ben fiddled with soldering joints and screwing down valve holders and winding coils, and he *kibbitzed*. A *kibbitzer* stands over your shoulder when you're playing cards and shakes his head and says " Ts-ts-ts-ts " whenever you touch a card. A *kibbitzer* expresses, but never in so many words, his disapproval of your slightest action. A *kibbitzer* can always tell you what to do. A *kibbitzer* is a punter's enemy and the bookmaker's friend, the man who won't let you play a hunch, the guy who won't let you be yourself, the fellow who appears to be the Oracle at Delphi and the wisdom of Solomon all rolled into one and who, if you follow his advice, will lead you quickly to the workhouse.

Lacher was a *kibbitzer*. King of the *kibbitzers*.

After a while he began to annoy the usually placid Ben. After a while longer he began to irritate him. Finally Ben grew angry—a most abnormal Ben state.

" All right," Ben shouted at Lacher, " do it yourself, then.

Go on, show me. Show me. Show me," thus anticipating by
many years the refrain of a song which was to be a big hit.

Lacher pursed his thick lips, rolled his huge leathery tongue
round them, peered myopically into the works and, laughing as always, began to apply solder to what we learned later
was the lead direct from the electricity into the bowels of the
set.

There was a blinding flash, a dull rumble, everyone ducked,
the room was hit by a storm of flying objects and, when we
all finally straightened up, the set had disintegrated. And
Lacher was living up to his name. Laughing.

My brother Ben, viewing the end of hours of painstaking
work, the shattering of his hopes, and anticipating the wrath
to come of Charlie der Grosser, forgot himself. He hit Lacher
hard, right on his big bonk. The blow split Lacher's nose and
his spectacles. The eye crutches fell in many pieces to the
floor, the nose began to run blood and Lacher's eyes to flow
with tears.

Lacher stood there with the tears running down his eyes,
his nose as bloody as a defeated British heavyweight's eyes,
wire and vulcanite and glass slivers all over him, dusty, dishevelled, looking as though he had just come through a mine-
field and stepped on every mine—Lacher the *kibbitzer*, the
schizophrenic, stood there and laughed. It wasn't a nervous
laugh, either. He just saw the funny side of it.

This was too much for Booba. She picked up a frying pan
and plonked him over the head with it. She never had liked
him anyway. He turned round, looked at her with an expression of complete amazement—an expression which said, quite
clearly, *Fancy doing that! I've done nothing!* picked himself
up, dusted himself down, collected his odds and ends of spectacles, dabbed at his nose, went to the door, said "Good
night," and left us looking dazedly at him. We never saw him
again.

His was not a success story. He went through the war as
a Fire Warden and finished up as a shop assistant in a grocery
store. When I last heard of him he was still in the grocery
store, but he was no longer allowed to serve behind the
counter. He lugged sacks and parcels for customers in and
out of the shop. Still laughing, no doubt.

The dreaded visit of Charlie der Grosser turned out to be

just as awful as we had thought it would. He ranted and
raved. Demanded his money back—he had paid for all the
various items that had been blown ceiling high on a gust of
laughter—and he wanted his pound of radio.

Mother placated him. She promised him he would have his
set. And, within a week or two, his set was ready. And working. Mother had gone to a friend of hers who sold junk in the
Lane and been allowed credit to pick where Ben chose. My
brother found most of the items he wanted. Valves and odd-
ments which he had to buy himself were bought with money
subscribed by every member of the family.

Charlie der Grosser came again. The set was switched on.
2LO came through the big, bent horn loudly and clearly.
The big man was delighted. He paid Ben on the spot with a
crisp white fiver. It was the first time I had ever seen a five
pound note and it was to be a long, long time before I saw
another.

Ben and Charlie between them then carried the set and all
its appurtenances to Charlie's flat and presumably it worked
there just as well as it had done in ours. For Ben came back
proudly bearing another machine with another big, bent
horn. It was a phonograph which Charlie, in a burst of generosity, had given Ben. Charlie was one of those who kept
pace with the times and, like some American families I met
recently, discard the old in favour of the new by getting rid
of the old, no matter how practical, useful and attractive the
old may be.

Ben also had a dozen wax cylinders. We played them immediately. Booba listened attentively. When Dan Leno had
stopped croaking she looked at the machine, picked up the
cylinder, turned it round and round, put her ear to it,
breathed through its tunnel-like aperture and then pronounced, in a voice stating a basic irrefutable proof, her final
judgement.

" *Kleine menschen*," Booba said.

4   *Prozzies . . .*

Broughton Buildings was a hotbed of hot beds.

Immorality was rife. Knock on any door and it was five to four a five-to-four would open up to you. Kimono untied, big breasts flaunting, she would motion you inside with a leer of her scarlet lips. They always wore kimonos. Their lips were always scarlet. Their breasts big.

There were no orthodox Jewish prostitutes. Nor any from orthodox Jewish homes. A few might have been second and third generation Jew but were as Jewish in thought, look and action as Hitler's mother-in-law. Some of them were girls who had married a man with a Jewish name. Men about as Jewish as Nasser himself. It was among the non-Jews who lived in the Buildings that most of the prostitutes were to be found.

From an early age I learned to differentiate between prostitutes and whores. Prozzies were young, attractive, wore high-heeled shoes and swayed their tantalising hips in your direction. Whores were old prozzies, bags, with the marks of their riotous living scarring their faces, their bodies wide and ugly, their hips sagging, too big to sway, their legs—unusually thin legs underpinning heavy bodies—uneasy in high-heeled shoes.

We had a theory about whores. Any woman who had a huge bosom and heavy hips and big thighs and the slenderest of slender legs was suspect as a whore. Fat bags had skinny legs.

Prozzies were all right. They smiled at you. They stole into your dreams. They made you feel good. Whores were disgusting, ugly, foul-mouthed, diseased.

Booba and Zaida made no such nice distinctions. To them all the " bad women " (my mother's phrase) were *coorvahs*. To us the attractive ones were prozzies and the old bags were five-to-fours. The young ones could be had for a pound or two. The old ones for a glass of gin. Both did good business.

Alice was a young pro. When I was about fourteen Alice was no more than seventeen. I fell in love with her. She was by far the most beautiful thing I had ever seen. Like a young gazelle she was, lithe and lissom and willowy. I followed her about with my eyes, entranced by her red shoulder length hair in the then current Rita Hayworth style, fascinated by the slenderness and the shapeliness of those taut hips, stirred by some hidden depths I did not know, till then, existed.

At that age I was just about half aware of the secrets of sex. I had learned them in the playground yard and at street corners, and could not separate fiction from fact. Born in the kind of festering environment that I was, I learned later that I was supposed to know all about sex before I was able to walk. But it wasn't like that. At fourteen we knew perhaps more than most boys but most of what we knew was way off beam, distorted by vulgarity and vulgarised by distortion.

My friends, the little Syd we called Lanky, insisted one day in school that men and women " did it " like dogs. The class took sides. We were about fourteen then and none of us really knew. We had to go and consult the experienced Roger Bageot for the answer. Roger, who had been doing it with prostitutes since he was twelve, laughed and laughed till we thought he was going to burst.

He finally spluttered the answer and we had to rearrange our thinking. That was the way sex began to fall into place. We heard a truth here and a whisper there and we began to sort fancy from fact.

I am trying to prove that at fourteen my love for Alice was pure. Sure I dreamed about her. It is the age for dreaming. And anyway, I don't suppose she knew I existed.

Till one day she brought some gew-gaws from my mother's stall and forgot to take them with her and I had to run the cheap shiny baubles up to her top floor flat in the tenement.

I knocked. Timidly.

The door opened. She stood there in a slip. I dare not look. I kept my eyes on the ground and proferred the brooches with my hand, not uttering a word.

" Mrs. Alec's boy, ain'tcher? " I heard her say.

Then I felt her hand under my chin and she was tilting it up so that I looked steadily at her, right into those green eyes.

"C'm on, I won't bitecher." And she grabbed my hand and led me inside and sat me down on a green velvet armchair and knelt at my side and looked at me.

I wished the earth could open and swallow me up. That mouth, that soft curving scarlet mouth. That long white neck. And the way her white breasts peeped above the short slip.

"My, you're tremblin'. Do I frighten you, boy?"

I shook my head.

"How're old are yer?"

"F . . . f-fourteen—and a half."

"Yer 'avin' me on. Yer don't look more'n twelve."

Indeed I didn't. I was thin, pale, weakly, wore glasses, looked and was undernourished, far more twelvish than fourteenish.

"I'm over fourteen," I insisted.

"You're the clever one, ain'tcher?"

There was no answer required.

"Must be good to be clever an' go to a good school and learn lots of things and be differen'. You differen'?"

I shook my head.

"You *are* scairt of me. You got pretty sisters. Ain't you never seen a girl afore?"

"Not like you," I said, finally finding courage.

"'Ow d'y' mean?"

"So . . . beautiful . . . so lovely," I said.

Suddenly she threw her arms round my neck and kissed me. A tender sort of kiss, not on the lips.

Then she took my hand and held it to her breasts and suddenly one big round breast flopped forward and she put my hand on it, clenching my fingers around it, and she held me like that for what seemed eternity.

Then she did a strange thing. She let her arm fall and quietly, tenderly, she began to stroke my groin.

Red hot shafts of muscular torture shot through me. My body seemed to be on a rack, bursting to get free. Shivers ran through my entire frame. I heard myself gasping incomprehensible sounds.

She stopped. Just like that. Quickly flipped her breast into her slip.

"You're fourteen all right," she said to me. She shook her

head as if the magic had gone, as if she had just been through a moment of inexplicable strangeness which she was shaking off. She moved to the door to open it so that I might go.

I stood up. On faltering feet.

"I love you Alice," I said. I just had to tell her. She had given me the courage, the passion to say it.

She looked at me. There was silence for a second or two. Then she laughed.

I had been in love before a dozen times and I was to be in love again a score of times and more. And each time love did not die. Each time it was killed. Murdered. Annihilated. Love never died, for me. It was erased for ever by a laugh, by just such laughter as Alice was enjoying; by the way my beloved sat down; by some ungraceful action of walking or running that suddenly made her appear unlovely; and, when I grew older, by the way a female farted in bed.

I was in love with love, with the Sir Galahad idealisation of it; to me it was all things beautiful, all things holy even in the moment of desecrating that holiness; and the slightest suspicion of ugliness, uncouthness, ungracefulness, unfemininity could kill my love stone dead.

As I walked towards the door I had no more love for Alice. I did not understand then what her being a prostitute meant. I did not know or care. Yet my heart was breaking.

She stopped me by the door.

"I usually charge a quid," she said; "but seein' as 'ow you ain't workin' yet, I'll make it ten bob for you. Got ten bob?"

I shook my head. I didn't know what she was talking about.

"Well, when you got it, come up 'ere and I'll make a man of yer." She pushed me out, gently, and shut the door behind me.

The incident completely nonplussed me. I told Bageot about it next day. We were sitting in a corner of the school playground and when he heard what I was telling him he motioned me into the lavatories and, though we were far more likely to be overheard there, insisted on my telling him everything in those sacred precincts.

When I had finished he did not laugh.

"She's a prozzie," he said.

"What's that?"

" You don't know? You mean to tell me you don't know?"

" Prostitute?"

" That's right. So you do know."

" What do they do?" I asked him.

He looked at me blankly. " They take money."

" What for?"

"For . . ." —he bent over and whispered in my ears— " letting you fuck them."

" No!"

" That's right," he said. He was a big fellow with a big grin. He had light eyes and they lit up when he laughed. But now they were clouded over with thought. He had never met anyone quite as backward as I was in those matters.

" But why should you pay?" I asked. " Can't you get it anywhere for nothing?"

" How, Finney old boy. How?"

" Well, you fall in love and you get married and then I suppose you do it."

" But suppose you want it before you get married. Like I do, once a week regular. Like you did, yesterday. That's what you wanted, you know. And she felt it. What do you do then, eh?"

" I suppose you try and forget about it, Baggy."

" Forget about it? Forget about it! You can't forget about it. That's what makes the world go round, my son. You don't forget about it. You do something about it."

" Like what?"

" What would you do?"

" Me? I'd try and fall in love with a girl and make her fall in love with me and then we could do it together."

" Yeh. Sure. An' she'd have a flippin' kid. Oooooh, that *is* clever, Finneyboychik."

" Yes." I remembered the affair with Wendy Tuppness and winced.

I saw what he meant. There were two things which, as we grew older, were to keep some of us pure. Not not wanting sex—we wanted it madly; but twin fear of consequences. One, you made the girl pregnant. Or, two, you got the pox. These, and not scruples, were the twin swords of Damocles we hesitated to bring crashing down upon us.

" So what do you do, eh? I'll tell you. You go to a prozzie, like your Alice, and you pay her and you have it off. No more worries. No more wet dreams. Simple."

" You can't get a kid? "

" No. She takes care of that. She knows how to prevent 'em. You don't have to worry about that one jot. Not one tittle little jot."

" And what about a dose? "

" Now that's something different. You gotta go with a clean one. The clean ones are safe enough. They take precautions and all that. Spray themselves with antiseptics before and after. Spray you. Then, if you wear a french letter, you're practically a hundred per cent sure."

" Not one *hundred* per cent? "

He shook his head.

" You can never be one hundred per cent sure. But you have to take a chance or bust. You can even go mad. Now that's worse than taking a chance ain't it? "

" And if you get it? "

" You *won't* get it."

" But if you do? "

" You *won't*."

" But just suppose. Just suppose."

" Then," he said, quite happily, " you go to the Lock Hospital and you get irrigations—they shove a tube down your prick. It's not that bad. My brother 'ad it. You get used to it. After about a year you're cured. There's no harm done really. And he only got it 'cause he took a chance—I mean a real chance, no french letter and he picked up a real bag, not one of them clean ones.

" Your tart Alice sounds all right," he went on; " now I'll tell you what we'll do. We'll go there tomorrow, straight after school. She'll most likely be in in the afternoons. They don't really start working till evening. What about it, eh? Eh, Finneymeladdie? "

I looked at him.

" I haven't got ten bob," I said.

" Don't worry. I'll pay. It's your commission for the introduction."

Bageot's father was in the rag trade. The son had all the right phrases ready for appropriate moments.

" I can't let you pay for me."

I was trying to wheedle out of it and he knew it. " It " was all right to think about, to dream about, to talk about; but only devils like Bageot ever went as far as doing anything about " it ". I was scared. He knew that too.

"Look," he said, " there's nothing to be frightened about. Everybody has to start sooner or later. I wasn't even twelve when I had my first. It was with the skivvy who came to clean the house twice a week. Nice young Irish bit she was. I was scared then I can tell you. But once you're away, you're away. You don't think about it when you're having it. You're only afraid now. Once you've got this little lot under your belt you'll be a different fellow. And from the way you behave you'll be a bloody sight better off when you've had your end away. Only one thing to remember. Never kiss 'em on the lips. They don't like it anyway. So that's a deal now. No withdrawing . . ."

He laughed. His finger prodded me.

I didn't see the point of that joke at all. Not then. About three or four years later I suddenly remembered the entire conversation, word for word, and suddenly laughed out loud. Up to that moment I hadn't realised that he was being funny. I was so innocent that I honestly didn't know he was saying anything except what I took it to mean: you can't get out of this now.

And it was true. I couldn't. There are many things a boy can lose. Face isn't one of them. He has to be able to face his fellows with pride. If I wangled out of this I knew that Bageot would not spare my feelings. I'd be the laughing stock of the school.

So I played it my way.

" All right," I told him, " but I don't want a soul to know. I don't want it to get back to my mother, and if any of the fellows know, even Shorty or Harry or John (mentioning my closest school chums), the news will be out. You must promise not to say a dickie bird to anyone, not anyone. Promise."

" Okay, if that's how you want it."

I know it didn't suit his book. He loved to boast about his conquests. There had been a time in the past when most of us believed it was all talk. But proof of Bageot's exploits had

been readily and steadily forthcoming; and the time came
when we knew he told the truth, even if he did embroider it
a little in the telling.

The following day we hurried out of school at three-thirty
and ran down the Whitechapel Road and turned into Goolden
Street. I kept close to the railings that skirted the outside peri-
meter of the flats. My great fear at that moment was that I
would be seen.

We doubled into the top archway and turned sharply into
the entrance of the block of flats where Alice lived.

Up the steep flight of stairs we ran, past the front room; past
where old Toby kept a sweet shop in her front room; past
Gordon, the mad Highlander; past the flat where Paddy
Rourke lived with his widowed mother.

We knocked at the door. Alice opened it, looked at us, saw
the pound note Roger waved saucily in her face and motioned
us in.

She was wearing a tight jumper that outlined the upper
body provocatively, a tight skirt that showed the line of her
brief briefs under it, sheer silk stockings and the highest of
high-heeled shoes. She was the type to perfection. I didn't
know it then. But by the very next day I could tell a prozzie
a mile off. That's how fast education was acquired in the
Buildings.

She had obviously dressed to go out. Her handbag and
stringy fur collar were slung over one of the green velvet
armchairs.

Bageot shut the door and turned towards her.

" Okay?"

That was all he said. There were no preliminaries. He put
the pound note on the table, pushed her into the bedroom,
closed the door and left me standing there.

I heard sounds. Her muffled voice. His. The bed creaking.

In less than ten minutes he appeared, pulling on his
trousers. She followed him a few seconds later. Her long red
hair was disarrayed. Her scarlet lipstick was smudged. She
hadn't bothered to put her clothes on again. The red silk
Japanese kimono she wore had not been fastened and I could
see her right down the middle, half of each big breast, her
navel, and the curliness of the red-brown pubic hair.

The effect on me was not the one Rosetti is supposed to

have suffered when he saw his bride naked on her honeymoon. The sight of pubic hair did not scare me off for life. Indeed, as I remember, I thought it added mystery and excitement to the female torso. But something was happening inside me, something that was like a constricting force: I felt that my insides were bound in steel, that I was being squeezed by an inner force that wound up through my bowels right up into my throat and brought acid vomit into my mouth. I felt myself trembling. The truth was I was petrified.

Alice was saying: " Your friend's quite a performer, ain't he? He's 'ad a few in 'is time. Right. You next? Got your ten bob?"

" Come off it, Alice," Roger said. " It's ten bob each—a quid for the two."

" Oh no it ain't . . . Oh no it ain't. It was ten bob for 'im 'cause 'e was so . . . little. Not for the like of you, fellah."

For one happy moment I thought there was to be no deal.

" Don't bother, Roger. I can do without it. Let it go."

" Oh no we won't, Finneyboy. You don't know what you're missing. She's red hot. Here . . ."

And he put four half-crowns in front of her.

She walked towards the door and beckoned me in.

It was no use hesitating, not with Roger's palm planted solidly in the small of my back. A push and I was at the bedroom door.

I walked in, head buzzing, stomach turning, and shut the door. She lay naked on the bed.

I didn't know what to do. I just stood there. She got up and helped me off with my jacket and shirt and vest. I kicked off my shoes. The sweat was pouring down my face. Then she loosened my trousers. My hands were shaking so I couldn't undress.

She looked at me silently, obviously not seeing the expected reaction. She pulled me over on to the bed and I wanted to be sick.

Her manipulations this time succeeded only in making me feel physically ill. Her mouth on mine was hot and stinking. After what I had been told I was afraid of her lips. Her underarms smelt of stale cheap scent.

She pushed me away. She wasn't angry or anything. Just fed up.

"Please," I begged her, "please don't say a word to him. You can keep the ten bob, only don't say a word to him."

She sniggered.

"You are funny," she said. "I won't say nothing."

Then, as I began to dress with clumsy haste to avoid her searching glances—I could feel them burning—at the nether parts of my body, she said to me: "You're all right, you know. Nothing wrong with you. Nothing to get worried about. First time, eh?"

I nodded.

"It takes some men like that. I seen 'em. If I'd 'ad a bit more time I coulda worked you round. You'll be all right, see if yer won't. You come back to me agin, eh, an' we'll make it up to you. That's a promise."

At that moment I could have kissed her; and probably made the grade. They say there's no such thing as impotent men; only incapable women. It's true. And Alice was not incapable when she wanted not to be.

We emerged smiling.

Bageot embraced me as though I were a hero back from the wars.

I never went back to Alice or to any of her ilk and it took me long years before I shed my virginity. But the very next day I was already a man in my many friends' eyes.

As my grandfather would have said: I got a vitness for it . . . I got a good vitness for it.

Bageot was the best of vitnesses.

ON MY mother's stall outside the centre archway in Goolden
Street could be found brooches, pins, vases, glass dishes, flags,
ornaments, souvenirs of the coronations of Edward VII and
George V, mementoes of the funerals of Victoria and Edward VII, frames filled with sentimental Victorian pictures,
empty frames, damaged candlesticks, candelabra, incense
sticks, tops of old tables, marble slabs, lace collars, a few
shawls, many Spanish combs and fans, and a huge tray of
hatpins.

Hatpins, my mother always said, were her best selling line.
Hatpins were, of course, worn in those days. But sometimes
the assiduous manner in which women ferreted out hatpins,
the quick, furtive way in which they made their purchase,
the fact that my mother sold far more hatpins than there were
hats or heads in the whole of Stepney, the insistence by the
women that my grandfather should not serve them—all this
sometimes made my mother say: " English womens his crazy
'bout 'atpins."

Until one day.

A man came to the stall and asked my mother if she had
been selling hatpins. My mother sensed immediately that he
was something to do with the law. A private inspector or
some such. She called him Sir. I was the only other one present at the time, so I am never likely to forget the way the
conversation went or what developed from it.

My mother replied that she *had* been selling hatpins, that
she had been selling lots of them and that they were her best
selling line.

" Mitout hatpins, sir, mine business would not be it ha
business."

After a number of questions the man produced a long envelope from his pocket and from it a hatpin wrapped in

cotton wool. Gingerly he unwound the pin from the cotton wool and, warning my mother not to touch it, asked her if it had been bought from her stall.

Mother recognised it once once. Yes. It had been bought at the stall.

Did she remember who bought it?

This wasn't easy. It was one of a fairly common type. But she racked her brains and she thought and eventually she named three women.

" What was that last one called?"

" Bella Leshy."

" Bella Leshy." The detective repeated the name for emphasis.

" And why do you remember Bella Leshy in particular?"

" Her—she was mine best customer. She is halways buying 'atpins, sometimes two, three times ha week."

" I see." The detective went on writing, flipping over the pages of his little notebook as he rapidly filled them. Mother grew more and more perturbed.

Finally the detective closed his notebook with an official snap. He looked up at my mother.

" Do you know why she wanted the hatpins?"

" Now hain't that ha silly question for ha grown man to be hasking. Why should womens want it hatpins for? To stick hin their hexcuse-mes?"

Suddenly mother seemed to realise what the detective had led her to say. Her mouth fell open and she gasped.

" You don't meanter say . . . ?"

" Yes. I do. Abortions. Bella Leshy was giving abortions."

" Mit hatpins?"

" Don't sound so surprised. You said so yourself."

" But mister, sir, Hi was making honly mit jokes, Hi don't know it what Hi ham saying, Hi ham not heven thinking such ha thing possible, Hi ham honly . . ."

My mother was distraught.

" We'll have to see about that, won't we?"

I had been standing in a corner unable to make any sense of the conversation. Hatpins. Bella Leshy. I knew Bella. She was a good-looking woman of about thirty-five, blonde, upstanding, well-shaped, well dressed. She wore silk flowered frocks all the year round and she had the thin legs of the bag. But she was no bag—at least, I had never thought so; nor had my Zaida ever called her *coorvah*. Then I would have been sure. The old man had an unerring eye for fallen women.

I had always liked her. She smiled at me, always looked very prosperous and smart, and was polite to my mother. And I'd often seen her rummaging around the stall. I'd even seen her picking out hatpins. She never ran them through her hair as most other women did, but had a trick of pressing the point against the side of her cheek.

And now she was in trouble. But what sort of trouble? And mother was in trouble too for having served her. With hatpins. I couldn't understand.

The next day's papers were full of it.

ALDGATE WOMAN CHARGED WITH ABORTION.

I sought hasty elucidation at school and Roger Bageot was at pains to put me wise. I was horrified. This, I told him, was worse than venereal irrigation.

"Worse? It's one thousand billions times worse. It's murder!"

It's murder. That's what Bella Leshy was finally charged with. I read every word of the trial; I asked innumerable questions; I was a great deal wiser by the end of it. And Bella a great deal sadder. She got twenty years for manslaughter. Of women.

My mother was her staunchest ally. Said she was only trying to help. The blad'n doctors wouldn't. The blad'n hospitals wouldn't. Womens needed habortions. And Bella Leshy and people like her were doing women injury, killing them often, because those same women *made* people like Bella help them.

"Womens come to 'er crying their heyes hout and they makes 'er do what she don't want it to. And sometimes she don't heven charge them hany money. I know many womens Bella never hasked ha penny piece from."

Poor mother. She was always on the side of the fallen.

Bella Leshy died in prison some five years later. She bequeathed to us a son, Morry Leshy; a son who had no father and had been in an orphanage from his birth till the day he was fifteen, when we first set eyes upon him.

I say bequeathed. There was no bequest. My mother, when she heard about the boy, immediately took him under her wing; and when he came out of the orphanage he came to swell the total of homeless wanderers who made our home their own.

But back to the day the detective arrived at the stall. The traumatic event that followed seared itself on my memory for ever. When he left, my mother was shaking.

I led her upstairs. The flat was empty. Everyone was at work. Zaida was in *shool*. Booba was downstairs at the kitchen stove.

Mother sat down in an armchair and promptly fainted.

Ever since I could remember she had been subject to faints. They upset me. I used to stand in the background and watch with fear as the smelling salts were applied, her hands were rubbed, her cheeks pinched and finally she came round. With an audience of my brothers and sisters watching her anxiously.

I had never been alone with her when she fainted. I did not know what to do. She was sitting on a chair and if I left her she would topple out of it. She was a tall woman, well built, and I had the greatest difficulty in supporting her.

Scared to my wits I none the less managed at last to force myself to pinch her cheeks, to let her head sink down between her knees—though it was only with the utmost exertion I could bring her back to the sitting position.

Ever at the back of my mind when I saw her faint was the fear that she would not come to; and sometimes the fainting fits were so protracted that I thought my worst fears were realised.

This was an occasion when she did not come to quickly and I was beside myself with apprehension, wondering what to do. Should I perhaps let her slip gently to the floor and run out and call a neighbour. But I was afraid to let her go.

And then, when I had almost given up hope, she opened her eyes, looked at me dazedly and started to laugh.

There was only one thing I dreaded more than the fainting fits. This was the outburst of hysteria which usually followed them. We reckoned at home that if we got mother through one of her faints without any subsequent hysteria we had cause to congratulate ourselves.

And now she began to laugh. Terribly. Terrifyingly.

It was a maniacal, demoniacal laugh. It turned my bones to water. I couldn't bear it. It was horrible, horrible, horrible to see one's mother laughing like a madwoman, head thrown back, teeth bared and the wild laughter rising up out of the throat and filling the air.

Now I was truly petrified. What could I do? This was something we kept from the neighbours as though it were a secret shame. No use running for help. I just had to stand there, a boy of about fifteen, watching his mother acting like a maddened hyena, baying at the ceiling like a creature out of an Edgar Allen Poe story.

I had seen my brother Mark bring her round once or twice. I hated his doing it almost as much as I hated the laughter itself. But I knew then that I would have to do exactly the same.

And I drew back my hand and slapped her hard across the cheek.

The laughter ceased in a kind of reluctant gurgle. She looked at me, eyes wide with wonder.

She never remembered, after it was all over, that she had fainted or laughed. Sometimes she would appear to be wandering and would babble about my long dead father or about early days in Russia or, at night, would suddenly want to put on her hat and coat and go out to the stall which had long since been packed away.

How much of an act was this—an act before an audience composed of her own family? For she never had a bout of hysteria in front of friends or acquaintances, only in the presence of the family. I don't think I ever remember her fainting except when her own children were present. And never did she laugh lunatically before strangers.

This time, indeed, she did not start to babble. She looked at me quietly and quietly asked me what had happened.

I reminded her of the detective's visit. The reminder brought tears. She cried, but they were natural tears and they didn't bother me much. She would dry them soon and get back to the stall. And this she did.

She wasn't even called as a witness. Within a few days the same detective called to tell her she was free of all blame and she did not have to worry.

But I worried. Long after the incident of Bella Leshy had faded from my memory, in sudden daytime flashes of recall, in fevered dreams I remembered I had slapped my mother.

I slapped my mother. Hard. On the cheek. And it was as if I had self-inflicted on my span of living a wound which would never heal.

When all else had been forgotten; when memory faded and one grew into a sort of maturity from which an objective and detached viewpoint could be obtained; when the years rolled away and Bella was dead and Morry was dead and the stall was a dim shape in a grey world of long ago, even then I heard that slap and saw it and felt it.

I think I shall feel it all the days of my life.

6   *Catholic, Agnostic, Jew*

THE MOST loved person in the East End when I was getting to be a young man was Dr. Deacon. My mother was perhaps the most respected; my Zaida was perhaps the most popular; but Dr. Deacon was the most loved.

Strictly, he wasn't even a doctor. He had been. But, during the war—the first world war: the one that made no impact on me—he had helped scores of young men to stay out of the armed forces. This may sound like treason, treachery, unpatriotic behaviour, *lèse-majesté* and biting the hand that fed him. But he did it because, primarily, he was a man of peace and secondly because he could not resist the tears and pleadings of the people who came to him. He really was a softhearted man. He truly believed in the objections raised by his conscience against war.

He had been found out. Reported. Imprisoned for most of the duration. Robbed of his doctorate. Deleted from the medical register. He came out of prison to find a crowd of East Enders waiting to greet him—English, Irish, Scots, Welsh, Jews, Africans, Indians, West Indians and even Belgians who had lost homes and possessions in the German advance and had been evacuated to Britain, England, London and the East End. Even they did not want their sons to fight.

Doctor Deacon would have joined up in the second world war. He was not alive then, but I know he would. He was a fervent believer in liberty, the freedom of the individual, the right of man to worship as he thought fit. He had no sense of superiority: of his own public school, university education and upper middle class background over the uneducated working class patients he attended; of white over colour; Jew over Gentile; Polack over Choot; man over woman; Briton over foreigner. He was a total believer in total equality. I got to know him well when I was a student of sixteen

or so, studying for my matriculation, allowed to ask him
questions at any time on physics and chemistry, at both of
which subjects he had excelled in his university days, and encouraged to use his own private study, a libraried room full
of books, whenever I pleased. I played chess with him after
surgery hours. I became almost a member of his bachelor
household. I really knew him well. And I know he would
have been among the first to volunteer for service in the
second world war.

But the first left him cold. He saw it as a struggle between
rival imperialist régimes and he was having no part in it.

He helped those who came to him because he was
genuinely sorry for the parents who would have to lose sons,
genuinely sincere in his belief that he should not help anyone
to fight that kind of a war.

He was no money grabber. He seldom charged when he
knew that his treatment would constitute a hardship if paid
for in terms of pounds, shillings and pence. Yet someone gave
him away. Someone shopped him. And he spent long years
in prison.

He came out white haired and bowed. And the East End
was there to greet him. They had missed him. They had not
forgotten.

Once more his surgery was full. Doctor-shmoctor. What
did the East End care for medical degrees? Doc Deac, as
everyone called him, knew his stuff. He was a good doctor.
A conscientious doctor. A kind doctor. A good man. *Der
heilige goy*, Zaida called him: the holy gentile. For Booba
he was Doctor Deek-kveek, because he always came—
promptly—when called.

For my mother he was a friend and confidant. Here was
a man who could talk to mother at her own level. She had
studied medicine as a girl in Russia before changing to teaching. The intake of Jews into the medical profession was
severely restricted and so she had had to switch her choice of
calling. She was tremendously interested in medicine. And
he in her early background. They got on famously. He argued
medicine with her, for my mother would argue her point
even when on unsure ground; and he listened like a pupil at
the master's feet, when she discoursed on the Talmud and
Rabbinical teachings. In this sphere she was a past mistress.

Few rabbis alive could have matched her learning.

He respected a woman of intelligence who had been left a widow at the age of twenty-eight with seven children and both parents to care for and had had the courage to stand behind a stall in the Petticoat Lane and eke out a living from the sale of junk.

When I knew them both as friends my mother was still a most attractive woman, tall and splendidly regal; fair of hair, light of eyes, with high Slavonic cheekbones, and the skin colouring of a Renoir maiden. When she had been widowed she was beautiful, people said. Yet she had never re-married. Had sacrificed her life to her brood. True, she gloried in it. But it was a life of sacrifice one *could* glory in. True, she enjoyed being a triton among minnows when, in such as Doc Deac's company, she would have had to fight for the respect she had earned by her erudition in the East End. But she was entitled to all the respect she could get. She needed it. She doted on flattery. And she got it. She even got it from Dr. Deacon.

"A magnificent woman, your mother," he used to say. "A jewel of a woman. A wonderful person." And so on. He was full of praise for her.

I have no doubt he was in love with her. Many were. But I doubt whether he ever said so or even hinted it. He knew that women of orthodox Jewish stock as my mother was never married out of their faith. Certainly not when their aged parents were still alive.

He was content to see her and talk to her; and she, who never gave her love to any man after my father, enjoyed his company and revelled in the talk that followed.

"She's a handsome woman," he once said to me after they had been engaged in a violent argument and I knew then, even as a sixteen-year-old, that he loved her deeply and would never say a word to her about it.

He was a good doctor. He had a felicitous facility for accurate diagnosis and would begin to treat a patient correctly long before most other doctors would have known what to do. His treatment was sure and confident and, as far as I can remember, almost always successful. He had a paternal manner too, a bedside air that gave his patients faith in the treatment and trust in the doctor.

When my younger sister Lily had measles and the spots
went into the eyes and there was a risk she might go blind,
Doc Deac sat up with her all night till the crisis was past. He
sat in our two by four back bedroom and surrendered his
sleep and refused payment when, after the crisis had passed,
Lily grew well again.

He knew my mother could not afford medical fees. And
sometimes they appeared to be fighting over money. Mother
would press it upon him and he would persistently refuse to
accept the couple of half-crowns being tendered.

For years he was called to the abortions performed by Hatpin Bella when they had gone wrong. This didn't come out
until Bella's trial when he was brought up in court and was,
for a time, in great danger of being sent to prison again. For
a long spell.

It appeared that he was guilty on two counts. One, that he
was not a recognised doctor. Two, that he did not report the
abortions to the police.

His defence, brilliantly and defiantly stated by himself,
was that he was called to help seriously sick people who were
in danger of dying from peritonitis. It was not his business to
enquire where and how these women had fallen sick, but to
save them. When he had saved them he asked no questions.
When he saw that they needed even more attention, he summoned an ambulance.

He was asked if he never suspected that his patients were
the victims of a crude abortion. He said that of course he
guessed. But he had always thought these foolish women were
the victims of their own ignorance. He had never known or
even suspected that Bella Leshy was performing these hatpin operations.

Would he have informed the police had he known?

No, he said defiantly. He would have given Bella a good
talking to.

But they couldn't bring him to trial for what he might
have done. They could only censure him at the trial, not his
but Bella's, for acting as he did.

The more dangerous situation for him was that he practised
when unregistered. He made a speech which moved everyone by its sincerity. He said he had been given a gift by God,
a gift he had worked at all his life and was still working at to

bring nearer perfection. He could ameliorate suffering and
sometimes save lives. He would go on doing this for the rest
of his days. It was not important that the law had taken away
his right to practise. It was important that people still believed
in him. When distraught husbands called and literally dragged
him to the bedsides of their sick wives, when terrified parents
came to plead with him to attend their seriously ill daughter
it was his duty to go and see what he could do. He could not
and he would not send them away to seek medical help else-
where, especially as, in most cases, he was called only at the
last moment.

It was his duty, as he saw it, to go on doing what God, he
felt, had called him to do. Licences granted by human beings
could not take away this divine gift he had, nor prevent him
using it for humanity's sake. He had been trained as a doctor
and he was still a doctor whatever the book of rules said.
And as long as the people of the East End believed in him
and looked on him as their refuge in times of physical trouble,
so long would he continue to serve them. If the State saw fit
to punish him for this, so be it.

The judge censured him, albeit with fairness and kindliness.
He made no mention of the Public Prosecutor taking up the
evidence against Doctor Deacon after the trial was over and,
in fact, nothing was ever done about it. The newspapers and
magazines had given the case of Bella Leshy a great deal of
space and in that space the so-called illegal practices of Doctor
Deacon were not glossed over; but there was always more
than a passing reference to this kindly man. One paper called
him " The Saint of Whitechapel ". One magazine ran a feature
on his work for suffering East Enders. The Doc got a good
press. Maybe the law decided not to antagonise public feeling.

I know that for weeks after the Bella Leshy trial—The
Hatpin Operations Trial, as the press called it—mother feared
that the Doc would be apprehended, Zaida said they had
vitnesses against the holy doctor, Booba pursed her lips and
said he would go back to " goal " and everyone in the East
End was anxious and worried about Doc Deac. Only the Doc
himself was not afraid. What had to be would be.

Fortunately for the East End, no action was forthcoming.
The law ignored the Doc. The East End continued to

crowd his waiting-room and he continued to run, single-handed, a huge practice that seldom paid its dues. He could be called on at any hour of the day or night, he never seemed to take any rest at all, he would stop eating the meagre meal he had prepared for himself to go out on an emergency summons. He never spared himself. He never asked for payment. When he knew people could afford it—the bookmakers and their wives when they were in one of their lucky runs, the market auctioneer who cleaned up on a Sunday, the steady always-in-work tailor or furrier or carpenter—he requested a small fee. Others paid him when they were flush. Others, seldom at all. Some, never.

The Doc went about his work. It was his vocation. He treated it much as a priest, much as the Catholic Father Gregory of the Aldgate Mission to the Poor looked upon his own task.

Father Gregory and the Doctor were good friends. My mother introduced them and the Doc, of Quaker background, the Father, a fanatic about faith, and my mother, the free-thinking Jewess of orthodox upbringing, joined in the most turbulent discussions.

The Catholic Mission at the top of Goolden Street had been set up to convert immigrant Jews to the only true faith. As far as I know there was only one *geshmutter*, one apostate there, a smarmy, smooth-skinned Galician who lisped. Everyone called him Ginger Nuts. My Booba called him *Der Galither*, accenting the lisp. People often called him *Der Galitzer*, but my Booba's monicker was too clever. It was one that didn't catch on.

Galicia, as far as I could make out, was a province in Poland which had once been Austrian. Its people were said to be fickle. Ginger Nuts had either seen the light or decided that a regular job preaching for the Mission was better than near starvation.

Ginger Nuts went out into the market, set up an orange box, and began to preach. His fiercest heckler was Shlomka the Carman. Shlomka was a rogue who hated dishonesty, a shyster who abhorred tricks, a knave and a rascal who was blatantly knavish in all he did and could not abide underhanded ways.

Shlomka destroyed every meeting Ginger Nuts held. He

attacked him with cries of "Rubbish! . . . Rubbish!" which soon became "Lie! Lies!" which in turn became foul abuse. Four-letter words fell like hail upon the apostate.

The Ginger Man, unable ever to complete a single speech, would really start to lisp and Shlomka, big and bearded, his beard fierce and aggressive, would mock him, lisping with him till the crowd split its sides laughing.

Then Shlomka would haul the Ginger Man down from his rostrum and take him away for a drink; and in the pub the Sunday market crowd had the time of their lives listening to Shlomka baiting the lisping one who, in his cups, lisped till the spittle soaked his hairless chin.

No one had any time for the convert in my East End. Yet folk used the Mission a lot. Its medical section was superbly equipped and staffed by some very brilliant doctors. All those who did not go to Doc Deac, some because they could not afford to pay and did not want to abuse Doc's generous warm-heartedness, went to the Mission.

Even Doc Deac went to the Mission. If he needed any special drugs or the use of expensive equipment he found it in the Mission. But the East End Jews were much too fly to be taken in by the Mission's mission of healing. They knew it was a medical sprat to catch a religious mackerel.

It was funny, really. They went there, the orthodox Jewesses, with their *shaitels*, their wigs, on their heads and their children tugging at their skirts, and they sang—or pretended to sing, or mouthed Yiddish words to—religious hymns; they looked at the forbidden pictures and images all around and they bore the illuminated texts, the figurines, the oil paintings and the prayers with fortitude. It was the price they paid for free medical treatment—treatment which most of them swore by. Some of the most devout Jews in the district worshipped the doctors at the Mission almost as much as their neighbours worshipped Doctor Deacon.

Father Gregory used to tell the Doc that with a name like Deacon he ought to have been a pillar of some church. They met often round the stall, and would then come in and have a cup of tea.

The Buildings were slum; but they were like palaces compared with, say, the monstrously deformed habitations in Glasgow, or even with the decayed plague of most buildings in

Bermondsey and Wapping and West Ham. Broughton Building rooms were papered frequently by the owners. The Jewish tenants kept them as clean as they could. It was a losing fight against bugs, but there were no stained walls, no leaking ceilings, no rotting floorboards. You could invite people into your rooms and sit them down in comfort. The houses were well furnished. Jewish housewives are normally fussy about their furnishings, so there would always be pleasant curtains on the rectangular ugliness of window and a soft carpet or two on at least part of the floor.

The loo was down a narrow passage which served also as a scullery. It had a sink at the far end and a door leading off which led to the holy place. So that by some fortunate accident of planning the loos, though inside the flats, were as far from the living quarters as they possibly could be in a relatively small area.

We had two flats and therefore two loos, one upstairs, one down. We were rich and not so stinking either. When we heard about less fortunate people who had to go out into the yard to get their duties done or about those even less fortunate who shared loos, we thought ourselves very lucky indeed that we did not live in a slum. Maybe even the King and Queen had to share a loo. We didn't. We *were* well off.

We had no hesitation in inviting all sorts of people into our rooms. We were proud of them. The bugs were very kind and usually kept well out of sight. Downstairs in the basement flat an occasional rat would find its way in from the cellars outside into which all the muck heaps of the flats above dropped, but what was only an occasional rat between friends. In any case we guided Father Gregory and Doc Deac upstairs. Our downstairs flat was known only to near members of the family such as Morry Leshy.

We'd sit around and listen to Father Gregory.

He came badly unstuck when he tried to convert us.

At the finish I believe we nearly converted him. For, taking the cue from mother we, as we grew older, would join forces against him and plague him with our beliefs and our views and difficult questions that even he, in his knowledge, could not adequately answer.

It wasn't that mother picked him specially because he was Catholic. Much to Zaida's disgust and horror she had just as much fun with the Jewish rabbis who visited us from time to time. To my Zaida a Jewish rabbi was *that* holy it was a mortal sin to question him at all.

One of mother's favourite questions to the rabbis who believed every word of the Bible implicitly was: if Adam and Eve were the first people in the world and Cain and Abel the first children, how is it that the Bible tells us that Cain went away and married? Whom did he marry—a monkey?

They never did answer that one. She also went to great pains to point out that working on the Sabbath in the time of the Bible was far different from working in her day: that striking a light in those days was a painstaking operation, but that now all she had to do was pull a switch. And she didn't have to yoke oxen to the cart to take a ride.

She cut through all the trimmings that hedged the religion round and was so knowledgeable on Rabbinical expositions and additions to the simple law of Moses that she and the rabbis used to argue for hours.

They never made her an orthodox Jewess, despite the rigid upbringing she had had at Zaida's hands and, after much argument, they would often, in disgust, tell Zaida he had fathered a freethinker.

But the most enjoyable arguments were with Father Gregory. For while the rabbis used to lose their temper and shout to convince my mother or storm when refuting her arguments, Father Gregory never lost his round smile and chose his words slowly and deliberately to make his point.

The arguments used to start gradually and build up into a family group discussion. And Father Gregory would finish his tea and settle back in his chair and put his well-kept hands over his ample paunch and listen carefully to all we had to say. Unlike the rabbis he listened. He did not interrupt. So, when he started to speak, we listened too, thus learning by example how to conduct a good discussion.

Though he always said "We preach Christianity; Jews practise it," I think he was surprised to learn that Jesus preached nothing new. Chapter and verse were given him to prove that Jesus merely adapted what had already been said by the prophets and teachers before him. *Love thy neighbour as thyself*—the great Rabbi Akiba had used almost the same words. And all our injunctions commanded us to take

in the stranger and be kind to the foreigner without the gates.
Isaiah, Joel and Amos had fulminated against animal sacrifice.
And when one of the Roman overlords had commanded one
of our teachers to explain Judaism in one sentence he had
answered in the phrase Jesus made known: *Do unto others
as you would that others should do unto you.*

Father Gregory listened intently as we taught him that
Judaism was not the cold inflexible faith worshippers of Jesus
believed it to have been in Jesus' day; but that even when
Jesus was a child the more understanding Jewish sects were
already preaching a softened form of Judaism.

If Father Gregory had lived to see the finding of the Dead
Sea Scrolls he would have known that well before the days
of Jesus there were sects of Jews, the Essenes amongst them,
preaching what today would be called Christianity but was
then looked upon kindly as a too-advanced form of Judaism.

My sister Betty who could get impassioned about things
she believed in always wanted to know why if God was all-
powerful, all-seeing, omnipotent and everlasting he needed
another to do his bidding. Her thesis was that such a God
could have entered the minds of men without recourse to the
aid of a man in mortal shape. By Christians admitting and
believing that God needed help, her contention was that God
must therefore be assumed to be that much less of a God.
And this she found impossible to tolerate.

Doctor Deacon who had learned the history of the day,
wanted to know why the historian Josephus, visiting the Holy
Land not long after Jesus was crucified, found no one who
even remembered the man. Many had been crucified. Crucifixion was the standard punishment. But of Jesus and his
crucifixion there was nothing especial to make it memorable.

In his own country amidst his own people Jesus had, in
fact, made startlingly little impact.

And when Father Gregory answered that it was through
his disciples that Christianity began, the Doc countered with
the fact that they were those who had never known Jesus,
never known the Holy Land, never known a word of Biblical
Hebrew or Aramaic. Yet, thousands of miles from their
Messiah and his teachings, they began a new faith.

Father Gregory would say that all faiths grew by word of
mouth. "Faith grows from faith, my son," he once said. The

F

words still ring in my ears. And I would point out how Jesus himself never wished to found a new religion. That even after Jesus died his followers were still accepted as Jews; and that for a long time they were still Jews until finally they were dismissed or voluntarily seceded from Judaism.

My brother Mark argued that Christianity, as a religious code, would have happened anyway. Today's Liberal and Reform Jews were more advanced in their religious thinking than any Christians had ever been. Judaism had progressed with the centuries. Jesus accelerated the change within his own time. He was rather like the passionate Socialists of the Keir Hardie era, preaching a sort of " religion in our time " creed.

With many of these theses Father Gregory agreed. What he could not agree with, in any shape or form, was the suggestion that Jesus was anything but divine. He would have been shaken to the roots of his faith by the progressive Christian thought which believes, today, neither in the divinity of Jesus, nor in the Holy Trinity and not at all in the Immaculate Conception.

In vain did Betty plead her theory that a God who is God needs no extraneous aid; that a God who had to create a Son to do His bidding was that much a diminished God. It seems to me, even now, a good point.

Mother had a point, too. " Why, then, Father," she would ask, " did Jesus cry it hout hon the cross: ' O God, why hast Thou forsake me?' " This, mother would argue, was the cry of a mortal man in agony, not the cry of a divine being, of one who must have known, if he were divine, his predestined end.

And if Jesus (or even God) knew the ending, then everything Jesus did in his life moved towards that final predestined end. Jesus was, therefore, to blame for his final crucifixion. Why, then, did the Church blame the Jews?

This was one of the questions to which we never did get a satisfactory answer. All the old answers were trotted out— that, in the moment of agony, Jesus reacted as a mortal; that he believed God had forsaken him; that while on earth he could reason only with the limited, although inspired, thought processes of a mortal—none of them convincing. We had heard them before.

On the questions of Jesus' brothers, with mother quoting relevant passages from the New Testament to give her words weight, Father Gregory remained adamant. It had been a virgin birth. There could be no question of that.

Jesus was not an Aryan. He was both a Jew and a Semite. Father Gregory did not argue that point. Nor that he must have spoken in the current Aramaic, interspersed with Biblical Hebrew, rather than in the Latin and Greek that only the Hellenised upper classes knew. These things the Father granted. But on points of faith he would not budge.

We told him that the Bible taught that when the Messiah came the lion would lie down with the lamb. Peace would come to the world. Had the coming of Jesus done that? Had it improved relations between the peoples of the world? Was not brother still against brother? Then Jesus could not be the Messiah. And, of course, the Bible did not talk about a Second Coming. The first was to be the final one. Alexander Campbell's Second Advent, prophesied for 1866, had turned out to be a non-Advent. That was only one of the reasons why Jews could never accept Jesus as the Messiah. Certainly not as God.

And why had God picked that time to send his Messiah? The world was still young and comparatively unwicked. Why not during that first horrible world war we had just come through? Why not at a later and more depraved stage in human history? Why then? And in that tiny country?

(In the late thirties I raised the question again with Father Gregory. Hitler was at his worst. Millions of Jews were dying. Hitler, born a Christian, whatever he called himself, had brought unheard-of sorrow and misery to the world. Where was Christ? I asked the Father. Where the Messiah? Where the goodness, the kindness, the understanding that Christianity was supposed to have brought to the world? How had Christianity benefited the earth if after nearly two thousand years of its holding sway this sort of thing could happen? I was bitter at the time, I remember. And Father Gregory, although so sympathetic, could only say that God worked in His wondrous way, and that that way was not always apparent to us. But by that time I could no more tolerate blind faith. I disagreed violently with the Father.)

" The workings of God do not always make sense to us," Father Gregory would say. " Why should they? Everything is for the best . . . everything is part of a sort of divine jig-saw puzzle that only God will, can, and knows how to solve."

He and her father (Zaida), my mother would tell him, had a lot in common. Both were believers in a set pattern of events. Both had unshatterable faith in God's workings.

" ' God's in His heaven, all's right with the world '," I quoted.

" That's right. God *is* in His heaven. All *is* right with the world," the Father would answer. " I believe that to the very core of my being. I believe everything is for the best. And that those who suffer here will have it made up to them in the Kingdom to come."

But, we would argue, there will be no Jews in that kingdom. No Muslims. No Buddhists. No pagans. Yet there are better non-Christians in the world than many who are Christians. And suffering is certainly not exclusive to Christians. Why should only those who believe inhabit the Paradise of God? Only those who believe as you believe? Would you exclude the saints who are not Christians? Would you exclude our mother, for instance, from your segregated heaven? How do you justify a heaven that only Catholics may enter? This, I once told him, was a vile philosophy.

These were the sort of arguments that we threw at Father Gregory; that he tried to answer without succeeding. For, according to his creed, only the self-confessed and the Christ believers would go straight into Heaven. Wonderful people like Mother and Zaida and Booba and Joseph-the-violinist-Kauffman and Blind Manny and Uncle Lotting would be doomed perhaps to Purgatory, perhaps to Hell. Why? Because, according to Father Gregory, they were non-believers. But God had made it so. God, with His pattern. He had made certain people Jews and others Muslims and other Buddhists and others sun-worshippers. Having thus made them, how could He then punish them for being just what He had made them?

Another series of evasions. Poor old Father Gregory. He came to convert us and we could so easily have converted him. But for his blind unreasoning faith, we might have converted him, too.

Yet he continued to come. He enjoyed the discussion. Loved to play chess with me. Counted himself a member of the family. And even my Zaida, who abhorred all Christians on principle, liked this *galach*, this priest, because the priest respected Zaida.

For me, personally, Christianity has influenced me most through the work of Michelangelo. The emotive force of his sculptings, their living warmth, their tremendous sense of feeling, their deep inner revelations shine with the inspiration of the Godhead.

It was Father Gregory who, to his everlasting credit, first brought to my notice that passage by a Christian doctor drawn up in early thirties at the start of Hitler's reign:

"A Nazi, who has venereal disease must not allow himself to be cured by salvarsan, because it is the discovery of the Jew, Ehrlich. He must not even take steps to find out whether he has this ugly disease, because the Wassermann reaction which is used for the purpose is the discovery of a Jew. A Nazi who has heart disease must not use digitalin, the medical use of which was discovered by the Jew Ludwig Traube. If he has toothache he will not use cocaine, or he will be benefiting by the work of a Jew, Carl Koller. Typhoid must not be treated, or he will have to benefit by the discoveries of the Jews Widal and Weil. If he has diabetes he must not use insulin, because its invention was made possible by the research work of the Jew Minkowsky.

"If he has a headache he must shun pyramidon and antipyrin (Spiro and Eilege), Anti-Semites who have convulsions must put up with them, for it was a Jew, Oscar Liebreich, who thought of chloral hydrate. The same with psychic ailments: Freud is the father of psycho-analysis. Anti-Semitic doctors must jettison all discoveries and improvements by the Nobel Prizemen, Bàràny, Otto, Warburg; the dermatologists, Jadassohn, Bruno Bloch, Unaa; the neurologists, Mendel Oppenheim, Kronecker, Benedikt; the lung specialist, Fraenkel; the surgeon, Israel; the anatomist, Henle; and others."

(Later on he would have been interested to see *The Times* reporting ". . . the discovery of special powers of the sulphanilamide group . . . lies in a line which leads back directly to the pioneer researches of Paul Ehrlich and his pupils.") And no doubt he would have acclaimed the influence of Doctor Chaim in the work of discovery of penicillin; and of my first cousin, my father's sister's son, Dr. Colombek who had been voted America's greatest bio-chemist for discoveries leading to the understanding of how the body works.

But Father Gregory, for all his narrow faith, was a most tolerant man. He taught me the names of great Jews, pointed out the great contributions they had made to art and science.

Through him I learned about Heine, always one of my favourites, in Germany; Brandes in Denmark; the debt Britain owed to the born Jew, Disraeli; that France owed to Mendès.

I was a little surprised and at the same time delighted to learn that Bret Harte, the great American discoverer of the American scene, was part Jew, as was Palgrave, whose Golden Treasury I knew from cover to cover. That from Marcel Proust who founded a new school of fiction to Andre Maurois, the Jews had made their mark on French and world literature; and that the great Montaigne himself was the son of a Jewish mother.

In Germany, home of the terror, German Jews had perhaps given most to the world. In addition to Heine and Wassermann and Zweig there were Feuchtwanger, Schnitzler, Ludwig and Toller.

In the field of chess they had produced brilliant players. The then champion of the world was a young American. In the field of music they had lighted a candle for the world to follow. From Mendelssohn to Bloch through to the kings of jazz, Berlin, Gershwin, Kern, Jewish music had stimulated a deary world. And the world's greatest instrumentalists were, particularly in the field of violin virtuosity, almost entirely Jewish. Mischa Elman, Stern, Heifetz, Menuhin (and nearer today the Oistrachs, father and son, superbly and unassailably the greatest pair of violinists of any time).

Jews, the Father told me, had made the voyage of Columbus possible, not only by finance but by the skill of the Jewish cartographers of Mallorca. And there was a school of learning today which believed Colombus himself was Jewish. Jewish lawyers, Jewish authors, Jewish sculptors like Epstein (today, in America, a brilliant dozen more), Jewish painters (Chagall only one of them), Jewish politicians, Jewish scientists and particularly doctors had contributed to the world's store of learning and knowledge.

And heading a galaxy of mathematical talent, the incomparable Einstein. And though the Jews constituted only about one half per cent of the world's population they had provided twenty times that percentage of Nobel Prizewinners.

The Father taught me that Jews are walking advertisements. That a Jew can be good and accepted; but let him be bad, let him fall foul of the law, and his name, blazoned across the papers of the world, would make it seem that all Jews were vile.

" You have inherited a mantle of suffering," said the Father one day to me in a talk I shall always remember; "—a hard way of life; but that should make you all the more proud, and you have so much for which to be proud. For your people has made light of tortures that would have killed off most peoples of the world and, in spite of it, they have given new wisdom to mankind. Be proud of your heritage, my son. It is a noble one."

I remember my reply, even now. " Is that why you wish so much to convert us, Father?"

And he had laughed his kindly beatific laugh and patted my shoulder paternally.

Had I known then what I know now I would have told the Father that 5,000 babies are saved every year due to the researches of Ehrlich; that those born deaf can now learn to speak because of the pioneeering efforts of Péreire and Van Praagh; that Nathan Straus of New York introduced pasteurised milk; and Dr. Barnardo, of Jewish descent, established the world's greatest orphanage. For these facts I was later indebted to the learning and wisdom of another great Jew, Louis Golding, may he rest in peace.

Father Gregory knew all this. He taught it to us. We admired him for his tolerance. But I was always glad I had been born a Jew with a strong, simple faith to follow. Christianity did not know where it stood. Judaism had always stood firm as a rock about God. One God.

Doc Deacon and the Father used to argue most about the theory of self will. It was the Father's contention that men were given a free choice and could make what they pleased of their lives.

Doc Deacon once said: "What sort of free choice has a deformed pigmy born to a primitive tribe in the undiscovered jungles of the Amazon?"

The Father contended that even such a man would know, instinctively, the difference between good and evil.

The Doc would then argue to this effect: surely God knows what the future will be for the world?

Father Gregory would give him a reluctant affirmation.

And Doc Deac would launch into a tirade. He argued, as my sister Betty had argued, that a God, to be a God, must have foreknowledge: of tomorrow, next year, a thousand years hence. That future was mankind's future and therefore the sum total of the future of every living soul. God, he would say, must know what will happen to every single individual if He is assumed to know what will happen to all. And if He knows what will happen to every single individual, where does free-will enter into living? It is already ordained that a man should do or not do certain things, think or not think certain thoughts, act or not act out certain prescribed and set courses.

God, said the Doc, was myth.

Free-will, said the Doc, was an invention of religion to answer the one question that neither Christianity nor Judaism could answer: that a God, to be a God, must know the future; which meant the individual as well as the collective future, one stemming automatically from the other. That, therefore, if one believed in God one must believe in wickedness as well as righteousness, in evil as well as goodness, for God was responsible for it all.

The Doc was at heart a great believer; but he loved argument so much that he pretended agnosticism to counter the Father's unswerving faith.

But when Father Gregory brought into the argument the concept of the Devil we all took sides against him, even Mother. To everyone this was an incredible faith.

So the arguments raged. Jew versus Catholic. Catholic versus Agnostic. Agnostic versus Jew. Round and round they went and evermore came out by the same door as in they went.

Father Gregory, still fighting a lost cause, would say that mother's intelligence and gift of the gab would be an invaluable ally to the Catholic Church and that, with her loyal following, she could lead scores of ignorant and doomed, into Heaven. He offered her many tempting jobs, jobs in which we would have shared in a world of comfort then unknown to us. All she would have to do was talk. And preach the Faith.

Mother would laugh at him. She expressed amazement that after all these arguments Father Gregory should still be trying to convince her when it was apparent he was the one who needed a new religion. But he remained undaunted. He tried till the end.

The session would go on far into the night. My Zaida would produce one of the bottles of *schnapps* he kept hidden and he and Father Gregory, the only two drinkers, would finish the bottle between them.

Then, both shaky on their pins, they'd get up for my Zaida to walk Father Gregory home to the top of the street.

They'd go off, arms about one another's shoulders. Singing. There was only one song they both knew. Volga Boatman.

They'd rock up the street, arms wrapped around each other, singing Volga Boatman at the top of their voices, Zaida in Russian. Father Gregory in English.

Latecomers would stare. The policemen, who knew them both well, would smile, and Doctor Deacon would wax angry at the childish behaviour of two adults who ought to know better.

The Catholic priest and the orthodox Levite arm in arm singing Volga Boatman. Yo-ho ho-ho . . . yo-ho ho-ho. The memory of it brings laughter and tears.

As he grew older and more and more harassed Doc Deacon began to take drugs to keep him going. I knew it first because one evening, when I was playing him chess, I saw him go over to a cabinet and inject his arm. I told Mother. She was horrified.

I caught them arguing about it. The Doc shook his head sadly. He told Mother it was the only way he could keep alive.

One night a messenger from the Mission came running. Would we come at once.

Doctor Deacon had stumbled into the Mission and died in Father Gregory's arms. He had smiled, the Father told us, as arms and embraced the priest. And thus he had died.

The whole East End turned out for his funeral. Thousands lined the streets. The traffic stopped. Blinds everywhere were drawn. Peoples of all colours, all creeds, stood and wept.

A Saint was dead. My grandfather wept too. My mother would not be comforted.

About three years later the Father died. Again, large crowds, a big procession.

My Zaida turned to me and said in Yiddish: *When I go to join them, do not grieve. It will be a very happy Heaven. I shall sit with both of them on the right hand of God.*

It was the most memorable utterance of faith I have ever heard. The words are part of my living flesh. The orthodox Jew envisaging a Heaven that was for all. O, what a world of real love there is in those words. O, what a glimpse of Heaven is there to give us all faith. O, my beloved grandfather . . .

Baldheaded Bastard

WHEN MORRY LESHY came out of the orphanage he was
fifteen. My mother vouched for him and they let him go.
They didn't seem to mind that we were already ten souls in
four rooms. As far as they were concerned we had two flats;
and any family that lived in two flats, that could afford two
separate residences, could afford to keep an extra person. We
did afford it. We sometimes kept an army. But how, I'll never
know. What we could not afford was the space. Booba and
Lily slept in the downstairs kitchen basement. Zaida in the
stock-room behind that. All the boys in the upstairs front
living-room. Mother and the girls in the back room upstairs.
It was a squeeze.

Yet we often had Jerry Short the dancer sleeping there; or
the man who used to cry "Seddahn, seddahn" when he
wanted you to be seated or the gentle pock-faced Lewis or
one of the many other characters featured in *No Tears in
Aldgate*.

Now came Morry. A tall, thin, dark, saturnine lad who did
not in the slightest resemble his blonde vivacious mother
Bella. She was dead. She had died in prison. Morry did not
remember anything about her. Nothing at all. He had been
put in the orphanage when he was about six months old and
she had never bothered to visit him.

I knew how the lack of a father left one vulnerable, in-
complete, unprotected, shorn of affection. But I had Zaida.
My mother gave me little affection. She was a demonstrative
woman in all things except the showing of affection. My
Booba was far too occupied cleaning and cooking and
scrubbing to have much time to show the affection we knew
she felt for us. But I had Zaida. Morry had no one. Nothing.
No roots. No ties.

When he came to us I remember noticing his large, dark

brown eyes. They looked at us with blank astonishment as though they could not quite get us into focus; as though they had lately been staring straight into a giant searchlight and could still not see us through the residual glare which hazed the pupils.

His ignorance was profound. They had barely taught him to read and write at the orphanage. He was terribly shy, seldom spoke and seemed to be afraid of the company of human beings.

He was about my age and I tried desperately to get to him; but I could not pierce that shell of shyness. Imagine my surprise then when I saw him talking in the yard to Paddy Rourke, the Irish boy from the next block. Paddy was alive, alert, fun, a neat little bundle of vivacity. They seemed a strange pair.

Yet the friendship blossomed. As the days went by they were always together. And when he was with Paddy, Morry came alive too and began to talk.

At home however we could not get two consecutive words out of him. He ate what was placed before him, cleared the plates, never said anything was too much, never asked for a second helping, just ate and got up and went out. Or, if it was late, he went into the far corner of the room and studied.

As if aware of his lack of education Morry had begun to study. He studied the dictionary. Since he so seldom talked we never knew what sort of progress he was making. But one day I found a crossword puzzle in a paper. It had been completed. Crosswords were just then coming into their own. All the papers featured them. Everyone tried to solve them. This one was a difficult one. I asked my brothers if they had solved it. No. Finally, only Morry was left. And, scarcely believing, I saw him nod his head when I asked him if he had completed it. It was incredible. He had solved a very erudite, very difficult puzzle.

My mother found him a job as a lift attendant. It was in a big factory building and once the staff were in for the day Morry could look forward to long periods of inactivity. He was busy again during the lunch hour and then had almost nothing to do until everyone went home.

He had discovered the Whitechapel Library, my studied home from home, and he went to work each morning with his arms full of books borrowed from the library. These he changed frequently. He was a great word swallower.

He shared my tiny bed. He would push himself right up against the wall, face it, and fall asleep without saying a word to me. In the morning when I awoke he was gone. Now he was working he took sandwiches with him and we wouldn't see him until about seven. He would eat, go off to find Paddy, return at about eleven, sit in a corner if visitors were present —and when weren't there?—and go to bed. He was a member of the family and never a part of it. We couldn't get him to open out.

About a year after he had come to us he turned to my mother one night and said quietly: " I'm off to France to-morrow."

My mother looked at him as if he had gone *meshuga*. It transpired, after endless questioning, that he had taught himself French and wanted to work in France.

And next day he was away. He never even said good-bye to anyone. We didn't hear from him at all. Paddy used to get letters and it was through Paddy we learned that Morry was working in France. Guess at what? As a lift attendant.

We almost forgot him as the years went by. Suddenly, there was a knock at the door one night and Morry was back. An eighteen-year-old Morry, bigger, stronger looking, but still with those lamplit brown eyes and that reluctance to talk.

Paddy came over that night. Paddy was just beginning to feel the onset of the illness which was to kill him. But he was a famous personality now in the East End, in London and even throughout Britain. People had begun to talk about Paddy.

Morry and Paddy embraced. I had never seen Morry react or emote before. Then they sat in a corner and talked fifty to the dozen.

There was one thing strange about Morry though. He wore a French style beret and he never took it off. And that night he did not go to bed. He just stood in a corner all night.

And from that moment on he stubbornly refused to remove that beret or to go to sleep in a bed.

He was not the sort of person you could fire questions at. If you asked him one question too many he just dried up like a clam. My mother pleaded with him to tell her why he slept standing up, why he would not remove his cap, what was happening to him. He merely smiled a sort of Mona Lisa smile, inscrutably non-committal, and looked at you with his large luminous eyes, wide open and brown as the furthest depths of the forest, and said nothing.

Zaida was pleased. Religious Jews always keep the head covered. Zaida thought he had got religion. " *Loz im tzoofrieden, loz im tzoofrieden—er geht mitt Gott* " (let him be, let him be, he goes with God). Booba was less complimentary: " *Er is ibber 'n bottle* " (he's over the bottle—i.e.: he's loony). Alf, Polly, Mark, Betty, Ben, Lily—my brothers and sisters—and I, thought he was crazy, that he had some kind of a kink.

We asked Paddy. Even Paddy did not know why Morry acted so strangely.

And then, by accident, I discovered the secret. We used to go across the road to the Baths once a week. Morry and I were packed off together. We got adjacent cubicles. I had my bath, heard him coming out of his, and thought I'd clamber up on the rim of the bath and speak to him over the top of the partition. I looked over and he was just about to towel himself. I saw the top of his uncovered head quite plainly. He was bald. Bald as a coot. I watched him take some green ointment from a tin and rub it into the scalp. When the whole of his head was covered with a vile-looking green slime he slid the beret over it. He stood there naked with a beret on his head and only then did he proceed to dress.

It was all clear now. Before my feet had touched down on my own side of the bath I saw it all. Somewhere in France he had picked up a bug and had lost his hair. Some quack had prescribed the ointment and he was using it. But of course he could not get into a bed without making an unholy mess of the pillows. And since he could not very well sleep in a beret without questions being asked, he elected not to sleep in a bed at all. I knew my reasoning was right. Of course he could have told us. Of course we would have understood. But his terrible shyness prevented him. That and his sensitivity; for he was acutely sensitive, inordinately afraid of doing the wrong thing, scared of people, terrified of looking foolish. And rather than confess to something which sounded so trifling, he preferred to make a huge secret out of it and to shroud the whole affair in mystery and silence.

We left the Baths together. I did not say a word. At home I told the family and they were flabbergasted. But no one proposed doing anything about it and we just left things as they were.

Then Paddy died. And Morry went to pieces. For the first time he threw aside inhibition and restraint and, in his terrible grief, let the world see him as he might have been. He cried like a baby, he cried and he would not be comforted. And on the night that Paddy was buried he stood up before us and threw his beret to the ground and stood before us, his bald head glistening bright green and sticky with ointment and said: "What's the use, what's the use . . . what difference does my baldness make now . . . what difference does it make now if I'm bald!"

It didn't make sense. But I know what he was trying to say. His little secret so carefully, so ridiculously nursed, was of no importance against the all-important secret of death. His little foible seemed insignificant compared with the greatest of all catastrophes.

He walked about the house for a week with his baldness showing. Zaida said: "*Er kikt oys vie a galach*" (he looks like a monk). Booba said: "*Oy doss ooremehr yung*" (Oh, the poor boy!). He walked around with those big brown eyes filmed with tears and then he announced that he was off to Spain to fight for freedom.

He joined the Republican army and he never came back. Six months later we had a communication saying that he had been killed somewhere near the River Ebro in battle. He had won a posthumous award. Poor baldheaded bastard.

We sorrowed. And forgot him.

Baldheaded Morry Leshy who slept standing up. His mother died in prison. He never knew her. No one knew who his father was. Those big brown eyes, deep as woodland pools, gazing at you through a mist. That smile so quiet, so quiet. Morry, learning the dictionary, travelling, going up and down in a lift. Morry, making only one friend in all his short life. You call that living? You call that a life lived?

Who remembers him? Somewhere in Spain he lies, this

friendless soul who saw nineteen years of the world and then decided it was enough.

The Mediterranean sun beats down upon his last resting place by the banks of the Ebro. The olive and the lemon tree bear their fruits. The brown earth cradles him. No one knows where his grave lies.

O life that holds back sweet fulfilment from the orphaned and the silent and the despairing. O living that cheats a boy of manhood. O those dark sad brown eyes. Those dark sad brown eyes, always so full of unshed tears, so full of unshed tears.

8   *Irish Will o' the Wisp*

PADDY ROURKE lived with his widowed mother in the flat below Alice. Mrs. Rourke was a dressmaker. Alice and Bella Leshy and the ladies of the Buildings kept her busy. She bent all day over the sewing machine and worked untiringly to give Paddy the best she could afford.

Young Paddy was an average sort of boy. Slim, fair, not too reserved, not too boisterous, not a fool, not brilliant, he would have gone through life without exciting interest had he not possessed one great gift.

He had grace abounding. Today, in an age where, of all qualities, grace has suffered most, he may have had to struggle; but he would still have made a name for himself. For his grace was god-like.

What is grace? It is beauty in physical form. It is a loveliness of movement, a symmetry of motion. In those days when Berlin and Kern and Gershwin were making graceful, popular music, melodious popular music; when the dance was a patternwork of flowing movements; when men walked with dignity and majesty; when charm was not the phony thing it is today; in those days grace had a meaning.

You must not think that there was anything effeminate about Paddy. Oh no. For at an early age he showed signs of developing into a great soccer player. He could twist and turn and sway with a litheness and ease that dazzled. He ran with the smooth rhythm of a line of Tennyson. His movements were like the silky ripplings of a mountain stream.

He had grace. He was not good looking, but he was good to look upon. His eyes were wide set and light. His hair was mousy. His mouth was not well formed. His teeth were bad. But when he moved he was very fair to see. A joy. A delight. A poem. A lilting melody.

At seventeen he was taken on the books of a well-known

G

London club and before he was eighteen he was playing on
the right wing and the press were writing his name in big
caps and people were talking about him and they said he was
a certainty to be picked for England.

Ah, but he had such poetry of movement. You should have
seen him waltzing down the wing, tricking opponents with a
delicacy that was superbly arrogant, shoulder swaying his
way past defenders, running with that lovely balance that
was his birthright, maintaining perfect control, dribbling with
speed and skill, looking like a dream.

And then the final shot. The shot that came with such
power from one so frail in physique. Paddy shooting. And
the net shaking.

How the crowds loved him. How they roared when he
started off on one of his trilling, bubbling runs. There are
few players in football who can get a crowd up on its feet,
who can send an electric spark surging through thousands
to light them up at the same instant. Paddy was one of these.
He had the quality of genius. He had the indefinable gift of
grace. Ah, but he was lovely to watch when he moved. He
was a virtuoso of the football field, a music maker at play.

At home, in the playground where he had played as a boy,
he was the same charming Paddy. Soon he would be truly
famous. He was certain to win a cap. The club would move
him away to a house. He would have made it. And all by
reason of his abounding grace and skill with a ball. We were
all proud of him.

But while he was still seventeen getting on for eighteen he
was part of his background. He kicked a ball around the yard
and ran like the rest of us when the caretaker came hopping
by on his gammy leg.

In his block lived Alice and Toby the Sweetshop and
Gordon the Mad Highlander and Manny Field who was to
win a lightweight boxing title and go blind. There, in that
gaunt tenement poking its head up at the grey sky, lived a
bunch of characters who could make an encyclopaedia of
books and many greater films than any Hollywood has ever
produced. But who cares about them? They were, and are
not any longer.

It is a source of wonderment to me that people can cry
with the words of a book, weep silent tears in the darkness

of the cinema, sigh over a painting, drool over a piece of
music and yet have no feeling for life itself. This life of ours
in Broughton Buildings was real and earnest and none of us
ever shed a tear over it.

Nor did anybody weep for us. If they had, we'd have
thought them touched..It is only now, with the years sped
away beneath the bridges of Time, that one remembers and
weeps.

Through Morry, who struck up such an unexpected friendship with Paddy, I got to know the lithe Irish laddie better
than most. He had a cockney wit and a ready flow of fun.
We used to watch Ras Prince Monolulu in the market on
Sundays—he was our favourite—and the tall, then young
Abyssinian with the princely bearing and his cry, later to
become famous, " I gotta horse!" and his fine upstanding
figure, mesmerised Paddy. He felt that Monolulu had a
crowd-drawing quality about him and he had been told that
he, Paddy, had it too. He wanted to know how they were
alike.

They were not alike of course. But they both had magnet-
ism. Monolulu by virtue of his fine presence and his rich
resonant voice. By his accents and his never ending flow of
jokes. Paddy by his perfection of motion. By the effortless-
ness he brought to effort, by the beauty he brought to ordinary, everyday actions.

We would stand and watch Monolulu. He had a trick of
drawing the crowd by rolling a sheet of paper inside a glass
tube, holding it aloft and making writing appear on the paper
which, when opened up, tipped a horse. That one was for
free. Other tips he sold.

" I'd like to do that," Paddy confessed to me one day. No
one is satisfied with his lot. Aren't we funny—all of us?

One day we heard that Paddy was ill. We saw it in the
newspapers first. He was not playing on Saturday. He was ill
for a couple of months. Then one day he came down to the
playground looking peaky. He practised trapping. He threw
the ball up and tried to kill it as it bounced. I was watching.

" Throw me the ball," he begged. " Please."

I threw him the ball. He tried to trap it, brought his foot
down and missed. The ball rolled on.

This was not Paddy. He had been able to pick a ball out

of the air and seemingly tie it to the end of his toes. His control had been well nigh perfect. Now the ball was running away from him.

And it went on rolling away from him.

He never played football again.

I used to see him in the playground trying to run with a ball, kicking it weakly against the wall, moving around without any of the ease and grace we had come to expect from him.

One day he saw me and called me and asked me again to throw him the ball. He had lost all his skill. I threw him the ball again and again and again and never once did he trap it as well as any six-year-old kid in the Buildings could have done. He was perspiring copiously and I, too, was feeling the strain, but he would not give in.

"Throw it." And again: "Throw it." And again: "Throw it."

He could barely stand upright. His face was drenched in sweat. Still he called to me to throw him the ball.

And then, suddenly, he broke down and began to cry. The sobs came softly, tearing him apart in their anguish, convulsive sobs that were unbearable to see.

I helped him up the stairs. I remember how Alice, bless her, was coming down with a gentleman friend and how she stopped and gave me a hand and how together we got Paddy upstairs and there his mother took him from us, cradling her boy to her for all the world like a child cradles a favourite doll.

Alice had tears in her eyes. Mine were wet too.

Three weeks later he was dead. Leukaemia.

And Morry was half dead. For when Paddy died part of Morry died too. I am sure he did not want to live any longer. There they were, a couple of eighteen-year-olds, saying farewell to the days of living. True, they had never been wine and roses; but they didn't know that. They did not compare their lot with that of more fortunate others. None of us did. We knew we were alive and that life was good. We did not feel pity for ourselves. We only knew that life, the only life we knew, was good. There were no tears in Aldgate, amongst the young anyway.

It is only now, in retrospect, that those of us who survived can see how empty and grim and forbidding were the days of our youth. But then, in those moments of time, we were blissfully unaware that we could have been, might have been, should have been blessed with a larger share of life's abundance. We were happy. We never thought anyone could be happier. Perhaps they were not? Perhaps we were the lucky ones. Ignorance was indeed bliss. Who can measure happiness? Who knows what happiness is?

Morry was never happy. I don't think he would have been happy anywhere. But Paddy was happy. Paddy loved life. His every action showed it.

He was a shooting star. I am not punning. He flashed into brilliance and was hailed as a coming international and then he was dead. And in no time at all he was forgotten.

But now and then, when I'm at a football match—at Wembley or White Hart Lane or Highbury or Stamford Bridge—I suddenly see Paddy running down the wing and I find myself standing up and cheering as I used to do and people look at me as if I were crazy and I sit down.

The ghost of Paddy waltzes down the wing for me still; wherever I see grace and beauty and perfect co-ordination, wherever I see effortless skill and immaculate control.

Paddy runs the wing for me yet, flying past opponents, bamboozling them with that sinuous sway of his shoulders, that pantherish agility, that almost sensuous way he had of moving. Ah such grace, such grace abounding. There was beauty, there is.

And I see him again in all his loveliness, in all his poetic and rhapsodic perfection. And I stand up and cheer.

And I alone can see the net shaking.

9 *Shlomka, Itzik and Gordon*

THREE OF the most outrageous characters anyone could ever have known were Shlomka the Carman, Gordon the Mad Highlander and Itzik Foortzer. Three characters, long-since dead, who have never ceased, for me, being vitally and eternally alive. Three characters so bursting with life that even death cannot kill them.

They were a clan. A holy terror of togetherness who made the East End rock with their escapades. Though they often clashed with the police, they were not wicked men; they were big boisterous fun-crazy individuals who drank more than somewhere.

And drink went to their heads. Fast.

They all wore beards. Itzik was a Jew. Shlomka, who spoke Yiddish, a nothing—he'd never been near a synagogue or a church in his life. Gordon was a Scots Presbyterian. As a threesome they were as irreligious a set who ever saw daylight. The Three Jews people called them because they wore beards; but, long before the word gimmick was known, they wore these beards as a gimmick. The beards were short and fierce and curled up at the tips. Beard-wearing was the mark of their clan. Shlomka's was red, fiery red. Gordon's was fair, golden almost. Itzik's was ginger.

They did things together. They baited The Galician, the smooth-cheeked, sallow-faced apostate, together. They ruined his meetings and made his life a misery. Then they'd get him drunk in the pub and tease the life out of him.

One night they stripped him of his pants. And his underpants. And pushed him out into busy, bustling Aldgate with his boots on, coat on and a prayer book under his arm.

They just didn't like *geshmutters*, that's all.

Shlomka, the biggest and fiercest of the lot, was a coalman who used his cart for other loads. Itzik played spoons in the market place. And Gordon—well no one ever discovered exactly what Gordon did.

From time to time when he was roaring drunk Gordon would dress up in full Highland regalia and come down into the playground playing his bagpipes. Kilt flying, pipes swirling, he'd march round and round the playground with the kids following.

Zaida loved Gordon. And Gordon and his henchmen loved Zaida. They called him " The Old Boy ". They liked the black ferocity of my grandfather's beard. They liked his strength. His gentleness. The way he gloried in four-letter words. He was one of them, almost. Had he requested membership I am sure they would have admitted him into the clan straight away.

When Gordon played the pipes Zaida would stand there clapping his hands to a ritual thousands of years old. Then he'd go off into a *chasidisheh* dance, the traditional dance of the old Polish sect of extremely orthodox Jews who, when praying, shuffle around in a circle and clap their hands and chant bo-bo, bo-bo, bo-bo, bim, bom, bim. It is lovely to see: these old men moving round and round to a dance, chanting and clapping their hands to age-old music. Topol and Bass do it beautifully in *Fiddler on the Roof*. My Zaida could do it. To bagpipes swirling, played by a drunken Highlander.

Gordon had a pretty young wife. He neglected her terribly. To make some money she went out to work. And the work she elected to do was the kind of work that brought in money quickly. One day Gordon caught his wife in the act, *in flagrante delicto*, and he went berserk. He picked up the man and threw him down a flight of twelve stone stairs, then he went for his wife with a knife. Her terrified screams brought Zaida rushing to the scene and my grandfather was just able to hold the wild Scot back until more help arrived. No other man would have been allowed to hold him back. Not in the mood he was in.

The fornicator sustained four broken ribs, a smashed jaw and countless bad bruises. He was in hospital six weeks. Mrs. Gordon suffered shock. Gordon got three months in the clink. He was met at the prison when he came out by Shlomka and Itzik. The coal cart came too, scrubbed for the occasion and decorated with paper chains, paper lanterns and flowers, as well as with welcoming slogans. They drove the cart in triumph down Aldgate and Whitechapel, stopping the traffic, and then down Goolden Street to the wild accompaniment of East End cheers. Everyone liked the villains. They were such nice rascals. Goolden Street pelted them, standing there in the coal cart, with rotten tomatoes. All in good fun.

Mrs. Gordon disappeared. No one ever saw her again. Gordon didn't bother. He seemed to care little about anything except his friends, playing the pipes in full regalia, baiting the Galician apostate, and getting drunk. I'm not sure about the order. Getting drunk, should, perhaps, have come first.

Itzik talked in spoonerisms. And played spoons. He always greeted you with " Mood gorning " and if you asked him how he was replied " Wery vell yank thew." It wasn't an affectation. Like a self-taught typist who transposes letters because the mind thinks faster than the fingers move, so Itzik transposed his syllables. He just got mixed up all the time. He couldn't help it.

Much later on, at the outbreak of war in fact, Itzik was made an air raid warden. He was given a whistle and told to blow it when the alarm went. When the first night air raid was signalled, Itzik went running round the flats knocking at doors. Whenever a door opened he put the whistle in his mouth and tried to say " Air raid! . . . Air raid!" then he took the whistle out of his mouth and blew a long blast on his lips. He ran from door to door with a mouth full of whistle through which no words came and a pursed-up mouth through which no whistle came. He knocked at about half a dozen doors, growing more and more confused, and finally passed out across the threshold of the flat tenanted by Alice. She hauled him inside and put him on the bed.

When Mrs. Itzik found him there, lying dishevelled on Alice's bed, half-awake and perspiring, there was a bigger explosion than any the falling bombs made that night.

Itzik was married. Well married. His wife was a dumpy little woman who nagged the living daylights out of him. It was no wonder he sought solace in the company of Shlomka and Gordon and that they were the objects of Mrs. Itzik's unrelenting and unmitigated wrath.

He was always being told by Mrs. Itzik to " shut up! . . . Shut up!" He had been married a long time—he was about forty then—and the insistent orders to hold his tongue must have induced the spooneritis from which he suffered. He wanted so much to say what he had to say so quickly that he tripped over his own words. Everyone thought it was very funny. What with his mixed-up words and his farting all the time, he was quite a character. It was always our ambition to get Rumbles, the Club Champion Farter and Itzik together for a contest. Rumbles could go at will. Itzik went all the time. It would have been a contest well worth listening to. But it never materialised. Ah well, gone with the wind . . .

Twenty years after I had left the Buildings I got into a bus at Victoria and sat immediately behind Itzik. He looked the same, the ginger beard slightly streaked with grey, the firm shoulders a little bowed, but there was no mistake. I wanted to talk to him but he was talking himself. And he wouldn't stop. He was reading aloud everything his eyes saw—shop front names, window bills, theatre notices, advertisements, newspaper hoardings, hotel names, bus destination boards—everything in print that appeared within his line of vision. He was saying something like:

" Yuinness is food gor foo . . . Danley Sturham, Asnewgent . . . The Trousemap is Bondon's riggest lun . . . Rabour lebels meet Mime Primister . . . Fenty-twour bus for Rottenham Tourt Coad, Steadhamp, Tamden Cown, Tentish Kown . . . Sadets, the cow nigarette . . . Orance Loliver is puserb in his patest lortrayal . . . The Hosvenor Grotel . . . Sticvoria Vation . . ."

He went on and on and on, reading everything he saw, saying it aloud in tongue-twisting incomprehensibilities.

And then, suddenly—" Why don't you shut *up*?" he said, and went straight on reading aloud everything he saw. Without a stop, while the bus went on, passengers alighted, passengers disembarked, tickets were clipped, money tended, London roared by, he went on translating into mutilated sound every printed word that took his eye: names, numbers, notices, news, newspapers, the lot.

And suddenly, now and again, he'd stop to ask himself

the question, with a different inflexion, with a shift of emphasis—" Why don't you *shut* up? . . . Why don't *you* shut up? . . . Why *don't* you shut up?"

He never stopped reading aloud.

Passengers came on the bus and laughed. It was funny, at first. But, within a few minutes, they were staring at him sorrowfully. And, after ten minutes on the bus, passengers who had come on laughing were almost in tears.

It was pathetic. The whole sorry business.

And when, sometimes, he changed the whole tenor of his question and asked it plaintively, pleadingly, as though he were begging himself on bended knees—" Why *don't* you shut up?"—it made you want to cry. There was so much pathos in it.

There he was, the Itzik I had known, not the same Itzik, not letting wind any more but talking it; reading aloud all the printed words wherever they appeared and every now and then breaking off to ask a question. *Why don't you shut up?*

It was a non-stop performance of non-stop anguish.

When I came to my destination I noticed the little bus conductress looking at him as though her heart would break. Tears were running down her eyes. " Ain't it awful? Ain't it just terrible? The poor, poor man. Ain't it a bloody shame?" I nodded. Most of the female passengers were wet around the eyes. The men sat there glumly. When one Cockney had turned to Itzik fiercely and said " Why don't you shut up, then!" more as a command than a question, Itzik had merely repeated his words in the same tone, without the final " then ". And on he went reading aloud, spoonerising the printed word, the trabalengual torturer chastising himself with masochistic fury and then pouring salt on his wounds with a bitter question to which he had no answer.

Mrs. Itzik had done a good job. So had all the unknown people through unknown years who had laughed at Itzik's lapses of language and told him to shut up. All those millions of *shut ups* pilings up, one on the other, till the whole world rang with one voice and all that Itzik could hear, all that he was ever going to hear from then on was *shut up, shut up, shut up, shut up!* Till, to stop the deafening cry in his head, he began to read, anything, everything, any time, every time.

And still the question, the supplication, the request, the command came through. *Shut up!* Till, in an agony of self hurt he would crucify himself with the pathetic cry made on a kneeling tongue, on a genuflecting mouth: when with breaking voice he asked himself " Why *don't* you shut up?"

That cry to himself was one of the saddest I have ever heard. " *Why don't you shut up?*" said with such pleading, with such self-pity, with such an agony of suffering, with such a world of despair. O my God, why hast Thou forsaken me?

And the interminable reading. A whole world of print to read and only hours to do it in. Print inside the bus. Outside the bus. On buildings. On road signs. In electric lights. An ocean of print undulating before him. A whole universe of unexplored print. Read with an initial transposition of Squeicester Lare, Hondon Lippodrome, Starren Weet, Koots the Bemists, Couse of Hommons, Astminster Webbey, Cank Bate Rut, Maily Dirror, and on, on, on, never stopping. But the final question always straight. No spoonerisms here. No mixed up syllables. No inverted letters. No transpositions. Straight. *Why don't you shut up?* The only straight thing he ever said, the only words that were fully understood by his hearers. And occasionally the plaintive question, the cry from the heart.

Poor old Itzik. He made me want to cry. The world had done a good job on him. We could all be proud. Proud of all the Itziks we have mimicked or laughed at for so long that, in the end, they begin to live their laughter and become the joke other people see them to be.

Itzik, a casualty of life. Itzik, who had been such a funny man, such a lovable rascal.

I remembered him as he had been. When he had beaten spoons all over his body, tap-tapping a rhythmic tattoo to a squeaking gramophone, keeping a beat, performing with an incredible virtuosity and ambidexterity, rapping and rolling and rattling the spoons across his arms, shoulders, thighs, sides, till the audience roared its appreciation and showered his hat with coins.

Itzik still performing to an audience. Tapping a tattoo not on spoons but on words. Tapping not on his body but on his soul. Itzik crucifying himself in the bus and crying aloud to

God to have mercy on him in a doleful, heartbroken cry of
agony; asking himself the unspoonerised question, asking himself in a tone full of tears and suffering. *Why don't you shut
up?*

Less than a month after all this I read that a man had been
knocked down and killed by a bus in the Strand. It was Itzik.
They gave a full description and his right name—the name I
had known him by. He was alone in the world. No wife. No
kids. A policeman said he had seemed to be trying to read the
numbers on a moving bus. He was probably doing just that.

Shlomka would never have gone that way. Shlomka was
the strong man of the unholy triumvirate. The leader. The
boss man. Big, strong, aggressive Shlomka.

Shlomka was a juggler of lives, a permutator of souls. When
people could not pay their rent, when they needed more
accommodation, when the landlord was after their blood,
when they had been given notice to quit, when the roof
leaked and the walls grew slime and the rats ran and the bugs
bit, people went to Shlomka.

For a consideration he would move you.

He came along at the dead of night, helped you load your
furniture, your possessions, your family into his coal be-
grimed cart, and took you off to another abode and helped
you move in there. Closed doors were no bar to Shlomka. He
opened them. He kicked them in. If a flat stood vacant more
than twelve hours it was a miracle. Before you could say
Shlomka the Carman, to give him his full title, he had filled it
with furniture and tenants.

He was an incredibly fast worker. And an incredibly silent
and tricky one. You spoke to Shlomka in the morning and in
the early hours of the next day he was at your abode and ready
to move, even if you weren't. Everything was piled into the
cart. And you moved into the new abode with your furniture
black with coal dust, your linens soiled, your carpets be-
grimed and your family looking like the retreat from Dun-
kirk.

He was the first commando. He blackened faces and took
over new territory, enemy territory. And left you there to
consolidate, to settle it with the real tenants or the landlord.
He flitted.

The moonlight flit they called it in the East End. It became an East End tag. If you were in any sort of trouble people told you you ought to do a moonlight flit. Shlomka the Carman and his moonlight flit.

One night he moved two families into the same flat, piled furniture on furniture, human being on human being and was away before you could say *flit*.

The Cohens and the Jones found themselves sharing two rooms. Ten people. Lithuanian Jew and Welsh Chapel. My mother, as always, felt sorry for them. She took in the Jones brood, five kids all under the age of seven, sent for Shlomka and gave him a good talking to—and you should have seen how meek the burly carman was before my mother's tirade— and had Shlomka store the furniture in his coal black yard.

The idea was that Shlomka should find them alternative accommodation. But quick.

However, before Shlomka could get moving, even if he really intended to, the kids got chicken pox. Mother called in Doctor Deacon. Meantime the kids were dumped all over our two flats and we all had to give up our bed space and some stomach room to them, for the meals meant for us had to be stretched. I never know where mother found the money from to do all the charitable, unselfish acts she was always doing, but she did. She was a marvel.

Recovered from chicken pox they went down with measles. Mother, *Die Shreiberkie*, as she was known in the East End because she wrote letters for people in six languages, had to call on me to write letters for her in English to the local council, the Health Officer and the local M.P.

Doctor Deacon began to call again. When that man wasn't visiting us socially he was paying us a business call.

It was all of four weeks before the Jones family was ready to move, by which time my English-Yiddish had developed a pronounced Welsh lilt and Booba was calling the cheery Mrs. Jones, " Missus Jones-Lookyou."

Doc Deac refused payment. " Why should *you* pay?" he asked my mother; " they're not *your* responsibility."

The local M.P., the local council, the local Medical Officer of Health had not even acknowledged our letters. Shlomka was sent for. He was told firmly that the Jones family must be found accommodation. He listened like a babe to mother and promised to do what he could.

That same night the coal cart stood outside in Goolden Street and Shlomka came and carried three of the kids to it while the Jones parents gathered up their few belongings and the other kids. There were tearful goodbyes not untinged on our part at least, with sighs of relief.

The cart was already piled full of the Jones' few sticks of furniture, blackened almost beyond recognition. And Shlomka moved off.

Early next morning a distraught Mrs. Jones was at the door to tell us he had moved them again into an empty flat in the Buildings only to dump a family of Belgians on them an hour later.

Mother immediately sent for Shlomka who apologised for the mistake, said he was being overworked, did not know how it happened, that it would not happen again, and mother must give him some time.

We took in the De Warts. They grew lousy. We all grew lousy. There were six kids all under the age of eleven and they were under our feet wherever we went. In our beds. At our table. And we began to scratch.

Doc Deac came again and annointed us all with ointment till we began to look like Morry Leshy with green slime on our heads and green stains all over the pillows and the arm-chairs. And the Doc once again refused payment.

The De Warts were Catholics. This was Father Gregory's problem. We called him in. He hummed and he hawed and then he said he had a solution. And he sent for . . . Shlomka.

They were moved eventually into a flat in Stepney and we never saw them again. Those little De Warts must now be big growths.

Shlomka seemed to get away with it. He had a list of empty places in the East End and he moved families into them; and the landlords appeared to accept Shlomka's machinations. It did not matter much to them who paid the rent as long as it was paid. And if Shlomka's tenants paid regularly, the flat owners were not too particular whether or not they had paid their previous landlords. Besides, it saved them advertising the vacancy. They had only to whisper to Shlomka that they had a flat going and he would fill it. Or a house. Or a stable. Or even a back yard. During the process of transposing people Shlomka would often put families and their furniture into disused railway sheds or old warehouses. He had the entree everywhere. There were many who said he was in the pay of the landlords.

But he was a good soul. He never maliciously hurt anyone. And he was extremely deferential to my mother, if to no one else.

There was the time my Zaida was accused of stealing a pram. Stealing a pram? Zaida couldn't make out what it was all about. But the woman who accused him said a bearded man had taken it. She took out a summons and Zaida had to go to court.

Shlomka, Gordon and Itzik went with him. They were going to see the Old Boy got justice.

Just before the case was about to be heard the woman decided that it hadn't been Zaida after all. But the police would not let her withdraw the charge and it had to be heard.

The three rascals had primed Zaida. All he had to say was " Not guilty." It was the second time my Zaida had been in court and now he was familiar with it. It held no terrors for him.

He scorned the interpreter. When the interpreter began to translate what the magistrate was saying, Zaida kept cutting him short with loud shouts of " Not guilty."

The magistrate got rather cross. He began to speak to Zaida, personally, and before he could say half a dozen words Zaida interrupted. " Not guilty!" he shouted.

The magistrate shook his head. There was no evidence and he dismissed the case. The interpreter began to translate the words of dismissal.

Shlomka leaned towards Zaida and said in the Yiddish he could speak quite well but always professed he didn't know " You know what he is saying, Old Boy?" And my Zaida turned round and bellowed at the court " Not guilty!" turned and left the dock and walked out into the street.

We later discovered the pram. It was hidden in a disused shed that Shlomka had taken over. He was giving it, he said, to a woman in Stepney Green who had had triplets.

Father unknown, he told us, and gave us a big wink.

AT JOSEPH HASSID's house I had met Ashermaun. Joseph was playing imperishable music on the violin and the great Ashermaun used to come and sit at the boy's feet and weep.

Those who have read *No Tears in Aldgate* will recall the tragic tale of Joseph; how he went mad; how the world lost and forgot what the world's outstanding violinist had called "the greatest living talent the world has ever seen".

Within that story there was another story. Ashermaun had brought with him Milcovitch as his accompanist. Milco, as we all called him, was a solo pianist in his own right, a virtuoso who could fill concert halls in America and Europe, drawing crowds by the sheer magnetic quality of his own playing.

What had prompted Milco to accompany Ashermaun, physically as well as musically? He had no need to play second piano even to such a great fiddle as Ashermaun caressed.

I was a chess player. At Joseph's house we often played chess and Ashermaun and Milco joined in. They were very keen. So I was not surprised when Ashermaun invited me to the Savoy, where he had a penthouse suite, to play chess with him.

Ashermaun was then sixty. Milco about forty. I was sixteen, going on for seventeen. I learned to love both men. Ashermaun was a virtuoso veteran of the violin. He had played before the Czar of Russia when he was seven. He was the infant prodigy who had become a world famous maestro. It happens to few. Only to the very best.

He was a tubby little man, with a smile always at the end of his mouth and a pair of bright green eyes, so bright that, when you looked at him, you saw first the luminosity of those twin lights, sparkling like emeralds. His hair was short, white and grizzly. He had podgy soft hands. His voice had not lost its Russian accent nor its Yiddish undertones. His American twang blended delightfully with his inability to pronounce " th " and his habit, like my mother's, of transposing " h ". He was just like a cuddly bear and I often longed to hug him.

Most of all however he was, to me, only the second elderly man I had ever met who, in my estimation, could rank alongside Zaida, my grandfather.

I worshipped Ashermaun. I revered his talent. I respected him and admired him. I loved him as a violinist and I adored him as a man. He was gentle, sweet, considerate, had a droll sense of humour, very Yiddish, and could flare—as Zaida sometimes flared—into explosive anger which thundered, burst and died away almost as quickly as it arose. But above all he had a big heart. He was full of compassion, full of warmth. He showed his emotions in typical Jewish fashion and this un-English characteristic of uninhibited emotiveness has always appealed to me. I like people who are warm.

Milco was a tall, thin, pale man. A tense, quiet person; serious, sober. But he too could flash into fun and make laughter throw back its guffawing head in the most unexpected places. Strangely, he was entirely without ambition. He didn't want to earn fame or make money. He wanted only to play the piano; and the fact that his talent had earned him much fame and some money too proved that the quality of this talent was indeed high: it needed no pushing.

Ashermaun fathered him. There was a wonderful relationship between the two great musicians, a quiet interdependence which could be felt even by the most casual observer.

I used to go up to the Savoy after school in the evenings and play chess with them. We had some great tussles. Milco was the best player. His brain was sharpest. He and I would set to with Ashermaun looking on and feeding us sandwiches and drinks—he waiting upon us, upon me.

I learned why Milco had decided to come over as second string to Ashermaun when, in his own right, he might have been taking a similar concert tour as a soloist.

In reply to my guileless questioning Ashermaun told me why, one night. Milco was out. The story could be told. Fifteen years before, when he was twenty-five, Milco had fallen madly in love with a girl who had suddenly vanished out of

New York to return to London where her father was dying. She had received a telegram and had left a note for Milco saying she had been suddenly called away and would be getting in touch with him.

She never did. He tried to make contact; but she had left her London address. There was no trace of her.

As soon as he had then been able, Milco had come to London. Flora, the girl, had vanished. He learned from friends that her father had died and she had disappeared after the funeral without telling a soul where she was going.

Milco went to the Embassies and the travel agents and had a private detective put on the search. All that they were able to discover was that Flora had booked an air flight to India.

Enquiries this end came to a dead stop. Milco flew off to India, cancelling a concert tour arranged for him in Europe. In Bombay he learned she had flown on to the East. His time had come to an end. He could go no further that year.

The following year he flew to Japan and learned she had come back to London. He flew on to London and searched for her. No one he knew, no one she knew, had seen her. The police could not help him. She was British. She did not have to register her changes of address. He searched desperately, frantically. Advertised. Had private investigators comb the country for her. But not a word, not a clue.

Every year since then Milco had been back searching. The quest had become a part of his life. He lived for the three months in each year when he could come to London and look for Flora.

The love he had had for her had become a dull ache, an anguish of heartbreak. That's why he had never married. That's why, Ashermaun told me, he was so unambitious. Finding Flora mattered more to him than anything in the world. In fact, said Ashermaun, he had now to go on *not* finding her. It gave his life a purpose it otherwise lacked.

What was she like? Ashermaun showed me a photograph. A tall blonde with a sunny smile. Not beautiful, but radiant rather. She was a sweet girl, Ashermaun said. Everyone had liked her. Milco had met her after a concert. She had always been one of his most ardent admirers. She was about his age. They had fallen violently in love.

And that was that. Till one night we were sitting there

when there was a tap at the door and there stood a rather buxom blonde, smartly dressed but somewhat barmaidy, and she was asking Ashermaun for Mr. Milcovitch. The voice was sweet enough. The accents cultured.

At the sound of the voice Milco, who had just picked up a chess piece to move, froze, piece in air, hand above board, muscles tense. He dropped the piece, got up, turned round quickly, and then grew rigid.

"Laury!" She called Milco by his foreshortened first name.

He stood still and looked. She advanced into the room to meet him and just when she was about to embrace him he stuck out his hand and she grasped it.

We sat down and drinks were poured. Flora babbled. How was he? He looked great. What had he been doing? How was the piano-playing going? What was New York like these days? And then she mentioned a string of names, asking how each one was . . . how time passed, didn't it?

Milco kept gazing at her as if some strange creature from outer space had suddenly descended in their midst. The expression on his face was one of stupefaction. His search was over and the prop that had shored up his life had been removed. His world suddenly crashed around him.

It was Ashermaun who asked the crucial question. What had happened to her after her father died? Milco sat there like a deaf mute.

Oh, she had met this business man who owned a carpet factory and they had fallen in love and they had gone off together to the East, were married in Japan, and had then moved round the world, to London, to San Francisco, New Zealand, Australia, back to London, on to Paris, on to Vienna, back to London—life had been a perpetual jaunt. They never stopped longer than a month in any place. She had two children, a boy of twelve and a girl of ten. She produced the photographs. Milco looked at them as though there were an invisible film between him and the postcards.

This was the first time that she had ever been in London at the same time as Milco so she had to look him up, she just had to look him up, didn't she? Tomorrow they were off to the Bahamas for a holiday, rather like coals to Newcastle wasn't it? but this time they would rest there for about three

months and then Jacob, the hubby, would be off again to show
his wares to the world and buy materials, designs and weaves
from far-off places. She was very happy. It was a wonderful
life. The children were at school in Switzerland and they
visited them often. Switzerland was such a wonderful international country wasn't it? and the children were learning
languages and that was good, wasn't it? and life was fun,
wasn't it?

And all through this long harangue Milco sat impassively,
like a poker player who thinks he is bluffing but on whose set
face lies the hopeless look of one who has been dealt a losing
hand.

And after a while she got up to go and Milco attended her
to the door and shook her hand and the door shut and he
came back and sat down heavily in a chair.

Ashermaun and I looked at him. He sat in stony silence
for a while and then he began to laugh, not uproariously but
laughing as though he had told himself a secret joke. And
he laughed to himself for a while and then he got up and
announced that he was going out to get drunk.

" You very disappointed?" Ashermaun asked.

" Disappointed? I'm overjoyed, overjoyed. Can you
imagine being married to such a windmill of words? What
would have happened to me? And where's all her looks?
She's just a plain, dumpy woman. God, am I a lucky man. Am
I lucky? I'm off to celebrate. I'm gonna get good and drunk."

The act did not deceive us. Here was a man who had
wasted fifteen years looking for a vision only to find commonplace dullness. Who had loved and lost, and had so obviously
been glad at the finish to have lost. Whose whole purpose
in life had suddenly disappeared. Here was a man about to
have to build a fresh outlook on life.

It was a tragic situation really and we all knew, Milco knew
too, that this was not a time for laughter. All those years of
dreaming. All that love. For what?

Of course he must have always guessed that he would one
day be disappointed. He always knew that if he found her she
would either be married or changed by the years. But it
seemed to me that he had been looking forward for fifteen
years to the grand dénouement, to a Wagnerian climax with
the orchestra crashing and the elements raving like a mad-

man. He had been prepared for some gigantic explosion that would smash him and his long carried dream to bits and all he had experienced was a stupid little pipsqueak. It was bathos. Sheer bathos.

What can one do except giggle at anti-climax? And so Milco giggled. Instead of being heartbroken by a terrible finale that he could wallow in, masochistically, he had heard the end of the symphony played on a battered tin whistle with its notes plugged. It was a let-down. A tragedy with a trite ending. A drama that died. He had steeled himself for unbearable torture and had suffered . . . a pinprick.

I saw then, in a flash of perception, that Milco would go on being unambitious, serious, silent; would go on searching for what he knew not. And so it proved! He is still, today, a near-great who never quite made it.

So he went out, leaving us there, wrapped in our own thoughts, silent and saddened. And another story began.

The chair I was sitting in faced a window that overlooked the Thames. Twilight was falling on London. It was September. It had been a golden day and the sky still glowed with aureate splendour.

Ashermaun picked up his fiddle and, seeking solace from its power to soothe, began to play. The piece seemed to come spontaneously to him, as though it were the only fit accompaniment to the mood that both of us were in.

He played the Mendelssohn Concerto.

Mendelssohn as the sun was setting.

The twilight turned to indigo with shades of amethyst. The room darkened to mauve and he played by touch, caressing the instrument as though it were a dearly beloved, stroking it, fondling it.

I sat there and the river turned dark blue and pinpricks of light began to stab the darkness and the music engulfed me and there was magic and mystery and enchantment and agony and ecstasy and tears all around. Unshed tears that fell with the music.

The slow sweet cadences of the Second Movement tore at my heart. Ashermaun and Stradivarius. We are the music makers, we are the dreamers of dreams. Keats and Mendelssohn. The one dead at twenty-six, the other at thirty-six and both immortal music makers. Those whom the Gods love.

Joseph Hassid and Paddy Rourke and Morry Leshy and
David and Lily and Keats and Mendelssohn and the night and
the music and the stars twinkling now and the room wrapt
in its cloak of dusk and melody and the utter, utter sadness
of a sweet, sweet song.

There it was. The world's greatest violinist playing for me
alone. Fiddler on the roof. Delightful depression. Ecstatic
sorrow.

This Jewish predilection to depression is what has made the
Jews the most musically advanced race the world has ever
seen. It is this ability to feel deeply that has hurt us and up-
lifted us. The sensitivity born of thousands of years of per-
secution and inbred togetherness has made our hearts bigger
than most. Only a Jew could have played as Ashermaun did
that night. Only Oistrach or Heifetz or Elman or Menuhin or
Stern or Millstein or Hassid. Only a maestro of the violin, a
virtuoso of music. We do not produce middle-class schizo-
phrenics: we produce all class depressives and it is a medically
known fact that people who tend to feel so deeply hit the
truly great notes of life, the C-majors of achievement.

The night was lit by a thousand eyes. He bent over the
strings, vibrating with them, echoing with them, himself a
part of the instrument, he, the man, playing, he, the man,
himself an instrument, himself making music with every
pulse of his being.

Ashermaun playing. The violin sobbing. The night falling.
The Thames rolling black, velvet black against the star-
spangled, light-flecked night. Night with a background of
music. A deep velvet black sky. And over all the harmony.
Mendelssohn. The same music that had been heard almost a
hundred years before and had gone on being heard and would
surely go on being heard. This is true immortality. Immortal
as the night. Undying music. Sad music.

And the cadences rolled one and then the other, echo
touching upon echo, vibrato on vibrato, the notes pouring
melancholically sweet and nostagically unforgettable. A
paean to God.

Exquisite music, the food of love, that gentlier on the spirit
lies than tired eyelids upon tired eyes, plaintive numbers telling old unhappy far-off songs, ageless music. The world's sub-
limest art.

And there it was. That's all it was. Milco finding his beloved at last. His music turning sour. And then in the sadness of the moment the world's greatest violinist playing the Mendel-ssohn Concerto for me, for me alone, in a room at evening with the sun coming down over the Thames and the twilight turning to Tyrrhenian purple, royal and splendid.

There it was. A man and a fiddle and me and Mendelssohn.

Such infinite indescribable beauty.

Such ecstatic sadness.

There it was. The greatest single thrill my life has ever known. Perfection, truth, beauty—all the things I was to spend the rest of my life seeking—here in one divine, one inspired passing of time.

Keats said it. This music that filled the room was " The same that oft-times hath Charmed magic casements, opening on the foam Of perilous seas, in faery lands forlorn."

There it was. The most unforgettable moment of my living. The greatest moment of my life.

I WAS born to the sounds of fists flailing, feet scraping on the canvas and the count of One-two-three-four-five-six-seven-eight-nine-out! ringing in my ears.

All around me as I grew up were boxers, ex-boxers and would-be boxers. The old 'uns were those who had once been boxers. The East End never forgot them. These men, many of them mentally as well as physically disabled, were greeted with honour and respect wherever they went. The living fighters were living heroes. Them, the East End feted. Everyone was proud of the "boys". And the youngsters like myself dreamed of the days when one day we would be champions.

Champions like—and the mind is crowded with names that came tumbling—Danny Frush, Pedlar Palmer, the Johnny Brown brothers, Jack Hyams, Joe Bloomfield, Harry Mason, Kid Lewis, Nipper Pat, Phil Lolosky, Alf Mansfield, Harry Mizler, Kid Berg, Benny Caplan and so many more; not all of them champions in status but all of them East End champions.

In the Buildings lived Asher Gerson who was on his way to a championship when he was hit by a low blow and paralysed. He dragged both his legs behind him as he moved on crutches, arms moving, legs left behind; then the hip joints sweeping the legs forward to meet up with those still mighty arms.

People remembered Asher Gerson. What a clean fighter he had been. What a good boy he had been. What a fine East Ender he had been. He had earned the respect the East End gave him.

Poor old Asher dragged his legs behind him and people were proud of him. He might have been a champion. Asher made a living selling newspapers. His pitch was well patronised. All the bookies bought their papers there, giving him twopence or threepence for the then halfpenny papers. And Asher seemed happy enough.

The East End was a fairground of booths and every booth was a boxing booth. In the fierce struggle for existence boxing promised bread and butter—no jam, not in those days, except to world champions possibly—in a world where even bread was a luxury. The Jewish boys of those days who had not done well at school found in boxing the way to make a living. Many of them fought at the old Wonderland and later at the Premierland for a cup of tea and a bun. The greatest of them all, Kid Lewis, a world champion, started that way.

The Kid fought at any weight, took on any opponent, was fast, skilful and ruthless. He was not only the greatest of the boxers to come out of the East End but one of the greatest lightweights of all time; and the world of boxing remembers him too. Not as a Jew but as one of the great British boxers of all time.

He was a skinny lad. He looked, and might well have been malnourished. My mother used to tell us how he would rummage around her stall when he was just a kid playing along the length of stalls down the street. Zaida used to tell us how he had often to cuff The Kid's ears to get him out of the way.

But he grew up to be a king of a boxer. And he even fought for a world light-heavyweight title, giving pounds away to the fabulous Carpentier, handsome idol of France.

In recent years I often saw The Kid at Stamford Bridge where he went to watch Chelsea regularly. He was old and big and heavy. And the heart cried a little at seeing in that image the young, spritely, eager, courageous and immensely skilful Kid taking on all comers. His East End had gone. His era had gone. Jewish boys did not have to fight for a meal ticket any longer. Only the good looking stupid clots became boxers and they made more money in one fight, having little ability and less brain, than the brilliant Jewish boys of the East End used to make in a lifetime.

I remember when The Kid won his fights. The East End would make merry. The Kid would ride down Whitechapel in an open car flinging handfuls of silver, riotously to the throng, being cheered all the way, lapping it up, loving every moment of the adoration people had for him, the way they loved him.

He gave treats to the local schools. I first saw Sophie Tucker at a school concert. Kid Lewis had brought America's Red-Hot Mamma to the Jews' Free School in London's East End to entertain the boys at the school where he was a boy.

He gave his money away as fast as he made it. He helped the sick and the needy. The East End worshipped him until he blotted his copybook by becoming political and joining the Mosley party before it had openly adopted fascism as its creed. Lewis stood for Whitechapel and finished bottom of the poll. Hero-worship does not include loss of reason. The East End did not forgive their Kid his fall from grace. And I doubt whether he ever forgave himself. It wasn't Whitechapel as a political constituency that he lost; it was Whitechapel as a living memorial to his past triumphs. But, over the years, the incident was forgotten; and today The Kid is still spoken of with affection. Champions of his kind don't grow on slum streets any longer. Today, anyone with a good profile and the dull wittedness to go out there and take everying an opponent will sling at your eyes, your face, your guts, can make a fortune. And does.

Fortunes weren't made in The Kid's days. And even a living had to be fought for, carved out of one's living flesh, bone and tissue.

Kid Berg was perhaps next in line to the greatness that had adorned Lewis. Berg was a two-fisted non-stop all-action hammer-away fighter who didn't know the meaning of the word defeat.

He was England's hero more than once. He fought in America for world titles which he lost by hairsbreadth decisions. And he finally gave up and retired, only to find that purses had increased and he was missing something by not fighting—the money he needed. So he fought his way to a come-back; and then one of our great national dailies which had been wont to hail Berg as the great British boxer who brought credit to British boxing suddenly remembered he was hardly British after all and led their story of his come-back with "when this has-been Jewish boxer steps into the ring . . ."

I wanted to vomit. Go on, delude yourselves all you in-
tegrating with-it Jews. Go on, tell yourselves you're British
and proud of it. Go on, look at yourselves in the mirror and
flatter your faces that the last proud line of semitic bearing
has been etched out of your countenance. And then, when
you're truly British someone somewhere will turn round and
call you *bloody Jew bastard* and spit in your eye. It happened
to Kid Berg. It happened in Germany.

As long as you bring credit to the flag they will stand up
and salute you and forget your background and hail you as
one of their own. But overstep the mark ever so slightly,
even to the extent of growing old, and they will put you
back where you belong. So belong! Belong with pride; with
the pride in culture that made your people civilised human
beings when they were clawing their way up trees; with the
pride at what you, a tiny people, have given to the world by
way of music, art, science, yes—and boxing; with pride that
your people, alone of all the old mighty empires still exist as
a people. Belong! There is no one who can match your breeding, criss-crossed though it may be with eastern, middle
European and Slavonic strains. Even the noblest of them has
bar sinisters that mock their ancestry. Even the noblest of
them attained nobility by robbing and pillaging and acquiring
land that was not their own. Your own breeding is far purer.
The passers have passed. The integrated have gone. You, who
remain, remain with pride in a lineage that goes back thousands of years, with a sense of wisdom given you by ages of
scholarship, with a familial feeling they can't even begin to
feel. Your roots are deeper than theirs. You can afford to be
different. Belong!

But poor old Berg did not belong any more. The paper
sneered at him.

Harry Mizler belonged for a while. He won a British title
and everyone was proud of him. He had one unforgettable
fight against Gustave Humery, the tough French champion,
a fight that seared itself on the memory by its red hot in-
tensity of courage. Mizler had taken a terrific beating and was
practically out on his feet when the last round was called.
He came up groggily, the crowd yelling " Stop it," Humery
straining for the kill. And with one last despairing blow he
caught the Frenchman on the chin and put him down for the

count to win a fight that had been given up as lost by all present from the very first round.

A nice boy, Harry. Quiet, undemonstrative, sporting, popular. I knew him well. He was a member of the same boys' club—the Oxford and St. George's, founded by the late Sir Basil Henriques—as I was. The club produced a number of fine boxers. Benny Lee had already won fame in the ring when Mizler was a boy striving to win the London Federation of Boys' Clubs boxing tournament. Also a member at the same time was Benny Caplan. Caplan the purist, the perfectionist.

Benny had the fastest, sweetest left hand since Jim Driscoll. He was a boxer, purely and simply, abundantly skilful, fast, accurate and graceful. But he lacked a punch. He could nearly always beat Mizler when they met, but he never did quite as well as a professional as Harry, although he fought a draw in Dublin with the champion of the world. I saw Benny pick punches off a Devonshire Club local hero, Alby Day, although he was giving away nearly a stone in weight. Alby had been built to heroic proportions by the power of his huge punch. One blow and they fell. Benny ran away, using the ring, moving out of reach, flashing that immaculate left hand now and again to score, while Alby, mesmerised by the speed and brilliance of Benny's footwork and lightning lefts, turned ponderously in the centre of the ring trying to pin this will o' the wisp.

Then, in the final round, with the fight in his pocket, Benny ran into a Day humdinger and hit the floor and was out. Cold. It was heartbreaking.

I used to take it to heart in those days. Today wild horses wouldn't drag me within miles of a fight. The game stinks. It is not only barbaric and ugly in the ring: it is vicious and putrid outside. It is a foul, ugly and depraved blot on sport.

There was a fight I saw in an East End ring when I was about sixteen which finally convinced me that boxing was not worth getting het-up about. A boxer was getting pasted all over the ring and the betting boys were laying ten-to-one and then twenty-to-one against him. He was staggering on leaden feet all over the place, taking punch after punch. His eyes were cut and his nose was streaming—in those days referees were not as fussy as they now have to be, not as quick to stop a fight the fans had paid to see.

All round the ring the betting boys were shouting the odds and I noticed three guys near the ringside quietly placing bets here and there on the forlorn hope.

Suddenly the pulped, bruised and tortured one leaped out of his corner after the end of a between rounds breather, walked straight up to his opponent, hit him hard and stood over him as the other fellow went down like a wet sack.

The battered boxer took one look at his sleeping adversary, saw that he would not rise within a minute let alone a sixth of a minute and, while the ref was still counting over the poor victim, ran to the side of the ring, leaned over the three guys who had been placing bets and yelled down at them, " I did all right, didn't I?"

There was murder round the ringside that night. Bet takers would not pay and bet layers demanded payment. Rival gangs tore the place apart. More blood flowed than the inside of the ring had ever seen. Broken bottles slashed. Razors flashed. I was glad to get away with nothing worse than a bump on my head where part of a broken chair had hit it. Then and there I realised that boxing was not a sport, had no right to be called a sport, and that I would never go near a ring again.

I broke that promise to myself only once. That was when Harry Silver, a brilliant young East Ender, appeared at Earls Court in his first big major fight. I liked the way Silver fought. I liked his skill, his grace. He had a touch of the Benny Caplans.

It was not difficult to keep away from boxing. Looking around the East End one could see pathetic victims of the game. Punch drunks abounded. Every other old time pro was punchy. Even those who had survived, apparently unscathed, were slow and slurring of speech, moved awkwardly like drunken apes, twitched, and were obviously far below normal in thought, co-ordination and behaviour. They were all apologies for human beings, subnormal and stupid.

I never knew a single boxer get completely free of the game without some mental or physical scars. Many, like Asher Gerson, suffered both. He dragged his legs and he dragged his speech and his thought processes dragged too.

But the most pathetic case of all those I ever met was Manny Field. Manny had been a fine lightweight—most Jewish boys seemed to make the lightweight grade—and had found himself defending a British title. He was ahead on points and his whole future looked brighter than it had ever been when the brightness faded. Suddenly. In a flash of blinding light.

He took a punch in the head, not a hard punch, and when he raised his head out of the clinch he could not 'see. He stumbled around the ring and the ref stopped the fight and helpers came in and led him away.

Doctors came and went as Manny sat at home, sightless. Finally a specialist. Verdict: damage to the optic nerve. Prognosis: probable permanent blindness. Treatment: none known. But . . .

But there was a French surgeon who had successfully operated on one or two cases like this. It would cost a lot of money—more than the up-and-coming Manny Field had ever earned.

Manny, on his way towards the bright lights, had done what many boxers before and since have done: gone to town, sampled the gay life, married the first attractive blonde they entangled with. Doreen was a chorus girl. Beautiful figure, blonde, common, tarty, true to type. Married him for the glamour, obviously. She wouldn't stay with him. The East End knew her kind.

But she stayed. And she went back to work. And she saved every penny towards the operation on Manny's eyes. Her money and the funds raised from a benefit tournament held for Manny, enabled them to make the trip to Paris and pay the surgeon for the operation.

Manny's younger brother, Mo, also a boxer, not quite as good as Manny had been, went on boxing. He had done the *right* thing. He had married a good Jewish girl, Ray, not a *shiksah* like Doreen. There were those who said that Manny had been punished because he had married out of the faith and that Mo would reap the reward of marrying a *balaboostah*, a real Jewish housewife.

Mo seemed to. After arranging a few fights in which he could cut in on the percentage, he set up as a bookmaker in his own right. Then he launched out and became a theatre angel, putting on leggy shows that did big business. He grew richer and richer.

Manny came through the operation satisfactorily. There

were anxious moments for him before the bandages were taken off and even after they were; but slowly the light filtered back into Manny's vision. After a week in hospital he could see. He was overjoyed.

He used to tell me the story as he stood in Petticoat Lane at his pitch. He sold liniment. He stood there in Petticoat Lane and sold rubbing-in oils for rheumatism, fibrositis, muscular aches and pains. He drew a big crowd because people still remembered him, and he sold his oils well. Doreen used to stand at the pitch and help serve the customers.

When the crowd dispersed Manny would talk to me. I heard the tale often. He smiled as he told it.

He'd come out of the hospital in Paris feeling like a million dollars. True, he'd spent all he ever made at the fight game, and more besides on the operation and the after-care treatment. True, he'd never be able to go back to boxing, and his dream of becoming a world champion was another of those dreams we all have that never come to pass. But he had back the sight he had feared he'd lost. A human being's most precious faculty was still his to use.

And he walked through Paris with a song on his lips, chirpy as a blackbird's trill. And he stepped off a kerb. And snap—just like that—he was blind again.

This time there was nothing they could do. Blindness was permanent. If only, he used to say, he had still been blind after the operation, it wouldn't have been so bad. The build-up of hope, the exultant elation when he could see again, and then the utter despair of the recurrence of sightlessness—this, he said, was what he had to learn to take.

He'd taken it. He accepted the fact that he would never see again. He forgot his terrible disappointment, the false hopes; he went out into the world determined to smile. And he smiled. He always smiled.

He was known in the East End as Smiler Manny Field or, simply, as Smiler. Everyone knew Smiler. Everyone loved him. His face was wreathed in a perpetual smile. When people approached him he would listen to their voices and then describe them in physical detail. It was uncanny how accurate his descriptions were.

He rated himself far luckier than Blind Pete who was born blind and did not know what colours were. He remembered the world, knew what colours were, how people looked. Even how his beloved Doreen looked. And, maybe he was lucky; for, for him, Doreen never aged. I saw her growing blousey and coarse-featured and ungainly; but for him she remained the lovely svelte dancing girl he had picked out of the front row chorus, long-legged and vital.

Sometimes I wondered if Smiler's life wasn't a sham; whether the smiles weren't all rather sad smiles; whether he wasn't doing a Punchinello act underneath it all. But I never caught him out. He smiled all the time, even when there was no crowd round him, even when you saw him, alone in the crowds of the Lane, smiling to himself.

Doreen stuck to him loyally. She amazed everyone by her loyalty to a blind man; by playing the game even when, in the first years of his blindness, she was still a very attractive girl and many rich men would have given her the earth to leave Manny and go live with them. She wasn't just sorry for Manny. She worshipped him. He was kind, she would say, and considerate, and loving and tender and— " Oh, just about everything a man ought to be " she would say, and your heart would lift with her joy in her man and you'd feel you were in the presence of something almost divine.

But as Mo went from riches to more riches, Ray was neglected and finally she left him. The East End couldn't believe it. A *shiksah* stayed with her Jewish husband who had gone blind, but a Yiddisher girl deserted her Jewish husband who had become very rich.

It didn't make sense.

I said this to Jackie, the youngest Field, a boy of about my own age and before I had time to think, I was in a fight, and in the crowd egging us on my was brother Ben, laughing all over his face.

Jackie was never to make a professional boxer. In fact, obsessed by his eldest brother's blindness, he studied medicine, specialised in ophthalmology and became one of the world's foremost authorities on diseases of the eye; but he had been brought up in a fighting family and he knew a lot too much for me. He gave me a pasting and finally stopped belting me when I cried " Quits, quits," which was the understood signal for ending a fight.

As a result of this fight I lost the leadership of the gang

which included Sammy Cockeye and Wendy and Asher Gerson's son and others, and found myself supplanted by Jackie Field. But I didn't mind. I spent a lot of my spare time at Manny's stall, helping Doreen to serve the customers, and I listened again and again to the tale of Manny's blindness.

In all the months of Sundays I spent in close contact with Manny I tried to catch him not smiling. But I never did. The nearest he came to not smiling was when we heard the news that Ray had been killed in a car smash along with the man she'd run to. And there were those in the Buildings who said " serves her right!"

BASIL L. QUIXANO HENRIQUES was a young man down from Oxford when he founded the Oxford and St. George's Boys' Club in Cannon Street, off the Commercial Road, in 1914.

B.L.Q. as he was first known, had found religion, in the shape of Reform Judaism, at a time when he had been plagued by doubts and was, it seems, in danger of accepting Christianity. Then he was introduced to the teaching of Claude Montefiore and saw the light. From then on his mission in life was to bring religion to the young Jews of the East End.

And side by side with Reform Judaism was an overwhelming patriotism, a fierce, uncompromising love for England and all that England stood for: sportsmanship, of the public school calibre; gentlemanly behaviour; no whining, no whimpering; dignity; quiet strength; and a playing-down of sex.

The Henriques family, after being part of the aristocracy of Spain had, in three hundred years, become part of the aristocracy of Britain. They were a great, a famous family. And good looking.

Basil was the handsomest man I have ever met. Tall, fair, with the classical features of a Greek God and the most beautiful speaking voice it has been my good fortune to fall spellbound by. When Long 'Un (another name of endearment) spoke everyone listened; and when he waxed eloquent, usually about religion, you found yourself hanging on every lilting, impassioned syllable. He could make music with talking.

My brothers were early members of the club. By the time I was old enough to join, the '14-18 war was over; the young man from Oxford was an ex-captain; and the club was in full swing.

Long 'Un had married the daughter of a Jew famed in

Hebrew scholarship—Loewe was a hallowed name to rabbis, Talmudic scholars, students, and those, like my mother, well-informed on Jewish history, law and tradition. Rose Loewe had already established a girls' club of her own in Betts Street, off Cable Street.

For a time the two clubs ran their separate establishments although the Old Boys shared the more commodious Betts Street premises.

Cannon Street was just a big house, converted. But Betts Street was a Settlement, with halls, cellars, gymnasium, kitchens and living quarters.

My brothers were *ganze machers*, big makers—important people—in the club by the time I joined. Betts Street was, by then, accommodating the very young as well as the over eighteens, and Cannon Street had been left with the fourteen to eighteen-year-olds only.

One day there was great excitement in the Betts Street club and its environs. The then Prince of Wales was due to pay it a visit. Strategic tumblersful of whisky were placed at different points of visitation and in due course the Prince of Wales arrived. A handsome young man but a dwarf compared with the towering six-and-a-half-foot Long 'Un.

I opened a debate before the Prince. He seemed to be very impressed. I was speaking, I remember, on the motion: *This club should be mixed* and I said both boys and girls would welcome it; both could enjoy the same conveniences. I remember how the Prince smiled politely. He asked me how old I was. " Ten, *sire*," I said. He smiled again. He had a very red face I remember, very light eyes, very fair eyebrows.

My very embarrassed elder brother, Mark, led him away to the first floor where a gymnastic display and a full glass of good spirits were waiting. By the time the Prince left the building he had disposed of at least half a dozen strategically-placed glasses of the best Scotch.

We had a lot of visitors at the club. Eddie Cantor came, complete with wife. A lesser member of the Royal Family. Cabinet Ministers. Writers, painters, millionaires.

Basil Henriques' work in the East End was being talked about.

Then came the great day when the late Bernhard Baron, the tobacco king, visited. At some stage in the proceedings

Long 'Un offered him a Players cigarette instead of one of Baron's own Black Cats or Craven A and finally got far less than had been hoped for. Instead of the expected hundreds of thousands of pounds, Bernhard Baron gave the club mere thousands. Sufficient to take over an old school, Berner Street School, and build a mighty new Settlement, but short by far of what he had confidently been expected to give.

The new Settlement rose like a landmark in a drab street. A synagogue was built into it. Every club night ended in prayers—a few words in English, a prayer in Hebrew—and religious occasions were celebrated in the synagogue with choir and solemnity.

The girls, under Mrs. Henriques—the Missus, as she was known—had one half of the building, the boys and men, many of these now with their own youngsters, the other half.

It wasn't just a club. It was a way of life. Boys who would normally have hung around the street corners; girls who would have spent their time at cheap dance halls; the despairing out-of-work during the long depression of the thirties, when I was just getting to be a young man; the youngsters from overcrowded homes; the orphans of East End storms; the waifs and stragglers—all these came into the club as nonentities and went out as men and women, proud of their country, their religion, themselves.

The club motto was *Fratres*; and indeed the spirit at the club, exemplified and fostered by the Gaffer, as he finally came to be called, was a brotherly one. Soon its members were spread all over the world and, when war broke out in 1939, throughout every fighting service, but they all kept in touch. One's first duty was to write to the club. One looked for the club magazine first amongst one's infrequent mail.

Run on the house system the club elected its own officers and house captains and began to run itself. Its football teams, for which my brothers played, won almost all the competitions which they entered; its physical training teams were the All-England Champions; at the club I won a medal for chess, the club winning the London Boys' Club Tournament, and I took the medal for first prize in the All-England Federation of Boys' Clubs Essay Tournament; the club's drama group gave magnificent shows to West End audiences; the club's boxers became household names. Talent abounded. The

Gaffer welded it together to produce a great, a famous club. It was a democratic institution, but he was always the man who held it together: a kind of benevolent dictatorship, really.

I remember at one officers' meeting a boy was hauled up for using foul language.

" What did you say?" asked the Gaffer.

The boy would not reply.

" If I have to repeat what you said I'll give you the thrashing of your life," the Gaffer threatened.

The boy, confident that Mr. Basil L. Q. Henriques, respected magistrate of the East London Juvenile Court, would never dare to utter the obscenity, smiled.

" You said ' fuck '," Mr. Henriques said and grabbed the boy and put him across his knee and administered to him a spanking he will never forget as long as he draws breath.

Camp was the big event. Annual camp at Goring-by-Sea, Sussex, on the slopes of Highdown Hill. There, qualities of leadership such as the Gaffer was always trying to bring to the fore, in the best public school tradition, and the ability of young men to get to know one another and help one another, to play together and work for a common cause together—these were given a chance to shine; a chance they did not always get in the bleakness of Berner Street.

Friday night the Gaffer held a Leonard Stern. These were prayer meetings named after a bright young Oxford graduate and club manager who had been killed in the '14-18 war. On a dark hillside, the boys holding lanterns, so that the night shone with a hundred eyes, the Gaffer would talk and preach —about God, faith, England, sex, behaviour, mankind. His subjects would range wide over a vast humanitarian and topical area and, in the darkness, everyone would listen. And then he'd pray and God seemed to speak out of the night. The dark hillside, the shrouded group of boys and the tall figure declaiming his faith.

He brought many boys back to God. A few to fervent patriotism. Some to Judaism. All to the club. At the hub of their lives was the club. They lived for it, going to it religiously every night of the week, playing for one of its teams at week-ends, taking it with them on Holiday to Highdown Hill, and living up to its precepts during their working hours.

I saw the club change many boys from layabouts into decent citizens. Many of them, starting out from the slums of St. George in the East, Shadwell, Commercial Road, Aldgate, Wapping, Cable Street, Whitechapel, became citizens doing good jobs. Some of them became rich. Not a few of them achieved scholastic honours. One or two became famous, and not only the boxers.

The Gaffer was always on at me to do more for the club. I used it, to quote myself in my words before Edward, Prince of Wales, as a convenience. I played table tennis, billiards, for the soccer and cricket teams, attended debates perhaps, but never really gave my all to the club. And the Gaffer saw it.

He knew of my success at school. I was the Big Chief there. He wanted me to do a repeat performance at the club. But that was the point. I had my fill of self-glorification at school. I had established myself there as a leader. I didn't need the club. Let the lesser mortals enjoy it!

The Gaffer, bless him, thought that all East End boys needed the club; all it gave them; all it stood for; that a boy born in the East End *had* to have the club make him a better man.

There was only one fault that both the Gaffer and Missus suffered from: they were patronising. Just a bit. Ever so little. But they were. She, I think, more than he.

They could not really imagine that any boy in their charge could be as mentally alert as they were, or that any boy born in the East End might turn out to know more about art and science than they did. Or that any of their charges were really quite in their class.

At the beginning, of course this was true. The first fourteen-year-olds B.L.Q. gave a club to, back in the 1914-1925 period, were mainly snotty-nosed slum brats who could only benefit from what the club taught them. But even they grew up. And became fine men and women. As time went on, more of us were already being educated (I am talking of the late thirties) and scholarships were being won more and more often by East End Jewish boys, and we were not entirely snotty-nosed, even then, young as we were.

The later club boys—particularly those who joined after 1930—boasted not a few brilliant youngsters who went on to do brilliant things. They were always in the Henriques' class, breeding apart, of course; though a Cohen is as well-bred as a Henriques any day.

I, unfortunately, was a little before my time. When, at sixteen, I found the Gaffer complimenting me on a piece of writing by saying: "You *can* write after all," I could cheerfully have sworn at him. The innuendo was plain. He conceded me the privilege of being able to write. He was amazed and surprised that one born in the East End could do it. But he conceded it, with his usual fair-mindedness.

The Missus was far more terrifying. She swept down the stairs and with a glance full of hauteur would shrivel up all the little boys who had dared to invade the sanctum of the girls' club for nothing more sinister than a chat.

She never gave me a glance. I wanted to tell her that I, too, knew something about music. It was her subject. She was very talented. She wrote all the lyrics to all the camp songs, fitting words everybody understood to tunes everybody should know. The tunes stuck that way. Club boys knew more operatic arias than most boys of their age anywhere in Britain.

Wealth and breeding had given them both—the Gaffer and Missus—a superior attitude which they tried hard to lose but which, for me, they never quite succeeded in shedding. They could not admit, even to themselves, that here and there among the many thousands of boys and girls who passed through their hands, there were better brains and more educated minds than they had.

I did not get to know the Gaffer as well as some boys did. As well as my brothers did. My brother Mark, who became honorary secretary of one of the clubs, knew him very well; was invited often, in company with three or four chosen favourites, to spend week-ends with the Gaffer at Sir Anthony de Rothschild's country house in Bucks. I never got to know the Missus at all. My brother Ben, because he could sing tenor, knew her well and admired her greatly.

One day I gave the Missus free tickets for a concert at which one of my violinist friends, a world-famous virtuoso, was playing. She accepted with grace. She was charming. Indeed, she is still one of the most charming and gracious women I have ever met. But, after that, she still never went out of her way to speak to me. I had been a member of the club for ten years or more when she called me one day and asked me my name. She didn't know my name. It hurt like mad.

There are members of the club today who will fight every word I have written with vehemence. For them the Gaffer and the Missus never were aloof. But for me, maybe because I felt myself their equal; and they knew it, and they knew that I knew it; and they resented anyone giving himself airs; and they were determined to keep me in my place—maybe, for all these reasons, I found them patronising. I admit it is the one fault I can bring against them. My inferiority complex told me I was as good as they any day. Yet for them, I felt, I was always a slum brat.

The traumas one collects in life! My club trauma is deep and scarred with resentment. But there is at least one other boy I know who suffered similarly. Struggling to prove himself he became a doctor, a brilliant one. But he still holds a grudge against the club for trying to regiment him into accepting his fate as an East End boy. For he, too, felt he was always being put in his place . . . way down.

Did I have visions of grandeur? When I got an Oxford scholarship the Gaffer, as an ex-Balliol man, didn't quite know how to take it. I think he was pleased when I finally opted to go to London instead.

Oxford was for Oxford-type men. London for the likes of me. At the time the strange fact is that this was true.

But my puny efforts to uncover feet of clay cannot take away from the Gaffer and the Missus the noble, the splendid work they did. He, with his patrician background and his great gift of speechifying, could have made a name for himself in politics though I think his high-grade honesty would have curbed his advancement. She, talented and queenly, could have been a famous musician. Both could have lived extremely comfortably, the life of the idle rich.

Yet they elected to forsake pleasure and sacrifice their lives to the East End. The Gaffer was knighted a few years before he died and they became Sir Basil and Lady Henriques. Man and boy I have known the Missus, young wife, woman, and now Lady, for all of thirty years. And in all that time the Missus and I have never exchanged more than a few words.

Der lahnger gott, the tall God, as Zaida called him, has raised for himself a perpetual memorial. In the street, lately

Berner Street, now called after him, Henriques Street, stands
a club to which thousands all over the world owe allegiance.
At the Gaffer's funeral the East End went into mourning.
Club boys stood guard over the coffin all night. Radio and
television paid tributes to him. The press carried long obituary
notices. He will never be forgotten as long as the Oxford and
St. George's lives—and it lives now in a myriad scattered
places all over the world.

My heart was heavy when he died that I had never truly
known him. That he had always been a little disappointed in
me. That he and I never quite functioned on the same wave-
length. But his life was big and majestic and splendid and
noble and I am glad to pay him tribute. He was a truly wonderful man and his was a truly wonderful life of sacrifice to an
ideal, the public school ideal of God, King and Country. Two
of those things mean precious little to me and of the third I
am not at all sure, not at all sure.

I wish I had the Gaffer's faith. If there is a Heaven he must
have a high place in it; for he was true, loyal, incorruptible,
unswerving in his faith to God and the country of his origin.
He never practised deceit and I am convinced that a lie never
consciously passed his lips. He was slow to anger, compassionate, kindly, proud, patricianly upright and straight as a die.
His blind spots were the blind spots of any saint: so much
concern for right that any deviation from an accepted principle seems like wrong.

Unlike some of the club boys who adored him, I never
loved him. But I respected him with a great respect. I was
afraid of him. And even more so of his wife. I felt she could
tear me to pieces at any time and I would not be able to reply,
not because I couldn't, but because my respect for all she
stood for would never let me argue with her. She made me
feel small. Maybe the fault was in myself?

He could be intolerant, but it was intolerance of anything
he honestly believed was wicked. He expelled a communistic-
ally inclined member who was a power in the club, a leader
of opinion, a house captain and a very fine fellow in every
way. This man went on to become a famous scientist after
taking a First at Cambridge, and, in his own sphere at least,
was as famous as Sir Basil. But he was never referred to in
any conversation at which the Gaffer was present. Having

no children he had doted on this boy like a son and was known to have suffered, through the boy, the greatest disappointment of his life. Asked once why he had no children the Gaffer replied simply: " I have thousands." It was true . . . of him, at least. He called the club members " children " and looked upon them as flesh of his flesh.

I once took my life-long friend Shorty to the club. Shorty was so called because he was six feet tall. The Gaffer, from six feet seven, literally looked down upon him and criticised the over-stylish cut of his clothes, the sharp edge of the double-breasted lapel, the then fashionably wide trousers, the gay silk handkerchief worn with a flourish in the breast pocket. The Gaffer hated ornamentation. He was anti-Semitic towards flash Jews. He didn't like Shorty's expensive clothes and Shorty didn't like him at all. Shorty did *not* become a member. Few grammar school boys did.

It was much harder for grammar school boys to take the Gaffer than it was for working boys who had left school at fourteen. The grammar school boys already had, at their schools, most of what the Gaffer was trying so hard to inculcate. To the working fourteen-year-olds he represented something new, visionary, out of their world, with his public school code and his ideal of service for the greater good of the community. Besides, the grammar school boys were wiser and not so much in need of influence to shape their lives. They could shape life for themselves.

Maybe that's another reason why I never really got to know him well. I didn't really need him. And I never had need of the Missus. They both liked people to need them.

I went to a few club camps.

It was the great event of the year for East End boys. Those who otherwise would never have had a holiday, never seen the sea, were able, on payment of a few shillings, to have a fortnight at Highdown.

There was an early rendezvous at the club, five-thirty a.m. So most boys did not go to sleep that night. They roamed the East End or stood around talking the night away. Even staying up a whole night without sleep was an event to which all looked forward.

Then the troupe would set out to march to London Bridge Station and thence entrain for Goring-by-Sea. Another march to Highdown, into tents prepared by the advance guard, and a quick change into shorts and singlets. Woe betide any visitor who arrived in full-length pants. Ceremoniously he was debagged.

Meals in a long marquee. Fatigue duty taken by each tent in turn. Competitions. The tidiest tent. The best spud bashers.

We had with us in our first camp a fellow who could out-fart anyone. He challenged everyone on the rambles we took every day and was undisputed champion. Every time he cocked his leg over a stile he could let go. He and Itzik Foortzer would have been well matched. He was a big, round chap, benign of countenance and character, with a huge sense of fun.

They used to put " jollop " in some of the food so that no one was constipated. One night Rumbles had it bad. We called him Rumbles for one obvious reason and also because he trilled his " Rs " throatily. When boys made him angry he would shout, more in jest than earnest: " I got frrree mallets —one to show, one to frrreaten, one to frrrow." It was a catch-phrase of many camps.

Rumbles was taken short that night. He farted so much that we drove him out of the tent. But the latrines were a long way off across half a field and Rumbles decided he'd never make it. Or, knowing him, I guess he never intended to try. He was a lazy, lovable lout.

When we had tidied our blankets and cleaned the inside of the tent in the morning, we went outside to tidy up the peri-meter, pick up pieces of straw, tighten or loosen ropes, smooth the grass. It was then we saw the neat pile Rumbles had left.

My brother, Ben, who was tent leader at the time, was hor-rified. " What do we do now?" he asked his tent, six of us. Rumbles said, " Leave it to me." The tent inspection squad was approaching. Rumbles smoothed the pile flat with a branch and covered the lot with grass. It was the neatest bit of camouflage I had seen. It took a war to find a way to beat it.

The squad arrived, duly headed by the Gaffer. They went in, looked round and expressed their satisfaction. They went outside and looked round. The Gaffer trod right into the camouflaged heap. A smell rose on the early morning air. The Gaffer looked around and said " Excellent. Ten out of ten," and wheeled towards the next tent, the shit adhering to the heels of both his white plimsolls.

Ten out of ten it was. We won the trophy that year.

My brother Mark, emboldened by fresh air, challenged Rumbles to a farting contest during a long hike to Arundel. Everyone counted, even the Gaffer. He was quite human. He could join in fun, even vulgar fun. It *was* funny. Every time they farted the whole crowd of two hundred boys kept score loudly. But Mark was beaten badly. He ran out of wind. No stamina. And Rumbles was declared undisputed farting champion.

Rumbles joined the navy on the outbreak of war and went right through the thick of it without hurt. He came back to crease us with his stories, particularly the one of the famous queer, an actor, who had decided he could serve his country and his own interests best by volunteering for lower-deck duty. Rumbles farted away at this half-fellow all the time they were together. And when the queer one complained Rumbles said: "Don't you like me making love, darling?"

Rumbles proved very popular in the Navy. He rose to the rank of mate. Today he drives a London taxi. I still see him and when I do, trust that his passengers aren't being subjected to extraneous rumbles not emanating from the exhaust.

Every day there was a hike. We walked. Sang camp songs, well-known tunes with words by the Missus. Lorries met us half-way for refreshment. Never were tea and cakes so welcome; never did they taste so good.

Back to camp. Supper. Sing song. Prayers. And the long tired sleep.

The Gaffer was afraid of sex. He believed that if boys were made to grow physically tired they would have no time to think about sex. But the East End boys didn't think about sex in camp anyway.

The Gaffer was probably afraid of the public school habit of pederasty creeping into camp life. But never was there the slightest suggestion of this in any of the camps I went to. East Enders just weren't interested in perversions. Queers would have been drummed out of the place. I am not saying this is right. Or wrong. I am saying that at this time queers were not fashionable and, in fact, most of the boys had never met one. I now understand homosexuality, and condone it.

But I must say, in all fairness that it has grown and so come out into the open in recent years that one is not quite sure who is what and why, and one sometimes wonders how much of it is real and to be pitied, or feigned and to be frowned upon. We never knew any queers then. The Gaffer, fearful that the bad habits of his beloved public school—he went to one of the two best in the country—might be copied, tired the boys out with walking and sent them back to their straw palliasses eager for sleep.

His other public school habit was his belief in the benefits of cold water. I hated this facet of camp. I hated the freezing cold sea. I was thin and I couldn't stand the cold. But everyone had to go in. Only a medical certificate could save one from the icy-cold rigour of sea-bathing on a Januaryish morning in July. And we have plenty of those in this clime.

I went in with the others, paralysed by the cold, shivering, watching the swimmers with envy, afraid to show the Gaffer how afraid I was.

I developed a sore throat. A very sore throat.

I went to the medical tent staffed by London Hospital students doing their bit of slumming. I was told there was nothing to be seen and was given permanganate of potash to gargle. I gargled and continued to bathe every morning.

The throat grew worse. I could not swallow. Even liquids would not go down. I tried to drink a cup of tea one day and it came running back through my nose. I was terror-stricken. I ran to the medical tent. They gave me a medicament to gargle and swallow, a black, iron-tasting liquid. I continued to go down to the sea in slips, to bathe and shiver, and feel terrible.

But one morning I was too ill to go. I lay in the weak sunshine outside the tent and watched the entire camp troop off joyfully for its early morning dip. I gargled and the gargle stuck in my throat. I was choking. I remember the pain, the terror. I fell on my face and clawed at the grass. I was helpless. I lay there choking, my fingers clawing the grass in agony. And then, suddenly, the liquid went down and I fell on the ground exhausted and lay there till the early returners from bathing found me and put me into the tent, to bed. My indisposition was not reported.

Next morning I was up and back at the familiar round. It

had palled. All I wanted to do was lie down. But the boys in the medical tent could find nothing wrong with my throat. Nothing at all.

Reassured, I resumed the morning bathe. The Gaffer said to me: "I hear you're complaining about your throat. All right, now?"

You see? I was *complaining*.

It didn't do to complain at camp. One boy who kept grumbling that his chest was sore had a huge mustard plaster stuck right across it. His chest was very hairy. When the time came for the removal of the plaster a gang of onlookers watched with amusement as the doctor ripped off the plaster in one Wimbledon-like backhand swing. The poor boy screamed as the plaster uprooted the chest hairs, leaving his skin as white and smooth as a babe's.

It just happened that this boy was shamming to avoid fatigues or something. Boys who grumbled about sore feet or blisters on their heels were told to "Walk it off!" "Walk it off" became another camp catchphrase.

It was true that in most cases the resort to blunt refusal to recognise sickness resulted in the sickness disappearing. But the public school tradition was plain. Englishmen did not complain. They bore their maladies with fortitude.

And I must be fair. If boys really were sick and ran a temperature, they were quickly removed to Worthing Hospital or into the sick bay tent and given constant care. But it didn't do to be not-so-well at camp. No one had any sympathy for the weakling.

I tried hard not to be one of those. But I did have a sore throat, a very sore throat and the young doctors-to-be could not even spot anything wrong. I grew embarrassed at going to them so often. They'd put a torch down the throat, look, shake their heads and say there was nothing to be seen. I knew they thought I was trying to get excused from the daily dip in the freezing ocean. The he-men, these young medical men amongst them, went dashing into the water every day, grinning as they raced past shivering mortals like myself who were wading tremulously into torture. They splashed us hard as they went by. In their wild exuberance to come to grips with the water they seemed also to show contempt for the poor, wee ones like me who just couldn't bear the cold.

It was the old British ritual. The old public school spirit. Cold water is good for everybody. Even for those who can't bear it. Rugger is good for everyone. Even for those who hate physical contact. So is boxing. So is racing across ploughed fields. A man's a man for all that physical endeavour. Good for you, and all that balls.

I felt this all the more keenly than most. For I was a good footballer and a competent cricketer. I could vault the horse or swing on the parallel bars with the best of them. I could run a sprint race as fast as anyone.

The club had once organised an individual competition to find the boy best at sport, indoor games and indoor activities. Everyone in the whole club, some three hundred and fifty boys, had been marked for their aptitude at football and cricket. Those who wanted to had entered for a road race around the East End. I came third in this, though I had never been road running in my life. We then entered a physical training session, a gymnastic session, and a boxing contest. We were given individual marks. There were debates at which we scored points. And there were also points awarded for essay writing, poetry reading, prose reading, and chess. I went in for a lark and won by a mile. I finished up streets ahead of the next boy as individual champion of the club. My brother Mark was very proud of me; but I gather I must have upset a few of the people who thought that the club was a way of life I didn't entirely go for. There were so many other boys who would have made worthier individual champions. They were far more representative than I of the club, and what it could do for Youth.

As Individual Champion I just had to go into the sea. I never learned to swim. Not then. Not for years afterwards. It wasn't till I was able to afford to bathe in the warm waters of the Mediterranean that I found I could enjoy water and then swimming came naturally. But that wasn't till I was much older. At camp I loathed the morning dip but went in. And I was determined not to let the doctors think I was always complaining; so I stopped going to ask them to do something about my throat. After all, was I not Individual Champion? Champions didn't get sore throats.

I dragged out the remaining days of my stay. I didn't eat, because the food wouldn't go down. I hardly drank, because most of the liquids I tried to swallow came back through the nose. My brother Ben, my tent leader, was very worried; but the medical boys had said I was all right. So I must be.

I thought I must be, too. It helped. I hauled myself off my palliasse every morning, joined in the stripped-to-the-waist public-school cold water washing ritual, went to bathe, and hiked in the afternoons. One very hot afternoon I even played football for the boys against the managers.

There's a lot to be said for believing you are well. I managed to carry on. But when I got home and Doctor Deacon, whom I visited, told me I had no business walking around, that I had quinsy and my temperature was nearly 102, I immediately began to feel very ill.

I went to bed. I became delirious. My temperature soared. My throat was now so bad that I couldn't talk. Only a thin little squeak emerged when I tried to say something.

Booba and Doc Deac nursed me. Sometimes I would wake from a fevered sleep to find the Doc sitting at my bedside. The ulcers on my tonsils were almost touching. The throat was practically closed.

I heard the Doc fulminating against the medical treatment at camp. He told my mother that any tu'ppeny ha'penny medical man, even a first year student, should have been able to see the soreness before it had developed into a dangerous quinsy.

Doc gave me tablets. Painted my throat. Came four times a day and often in the middle of the night to allow Booba to get some sleep.

One day he told me that if I were not any better the next day he'd have to cut. The danger was that the ulcers would burst and I would suffocate, unless they were cut. Tomorrow he would cut.

Tomorrow I was better. I suddenly began to sweat. The bed ran with perspiration. The pillows, sheet, even the mattress was soaked.

I had to be changed and sponged down every hour. The fever broke completely and the ulcers went. I developed a voracious appetite and ate almost without stopping. But Doc Deac kept me in bed a week longer and at home for a further fortnight. In all, the episode at camp cost me ten weeks of sickness and Doc Deac assured me I could have died; that, in fact, when I choked on the gargle in the deserted camp that morning I was within inches of death. It was in the days before the sulphonamide drugs had taken the danger out of quinsy. When I contracted the malady it was still a killer. Yet the medical students, some of them in their last year at hospital, had failed completely to notice a swollen throat with ulcers forming on the tonsils. Perhaps they didn't really look. Perhaps they thought me one of the shammers.

When I went back to club the Gaffer did not even ask me how I was. He had completely forgotten my " complaint ". He was a busy man and I bore him no grudge. He had many other more important things to think about.

But I never went to camp again.

Some years later, just after the second world war, I was asked by the club to sit on a quiz panel. I had written a couple of books by then and was a club boy who had made good. My brother Ben, who had established a small reputation as a singer on radio and television, was also on the panel. Completing it were Benny Caplan, the boxer, and my good friend David Jones who, starting as an office boy had risen to be head of publicity at one of the biggest film companies in the world and who is now, as I write, the respected and popular Chief Barker of the Variety Artists Benevolent Fund and has been honoured by the Queen with an order of distinction.

We four sat up on the dais in the big hall.

We were asked many questions and we answered them as best we could. Then a manager of the club asked the final question: " Would you say you owe your present position to the good things the club taught you? "

There was a hall full of boys and girls, about five hundred eager young ears tuned to the answers. There were managers there. And the big shots.

My brother Ben said the Missus had first encouraged him in singing. It was true. She had taught him appreciation of music, how to use his voice, had developed and fostered what was to become a lifelong interest in music. He praised her and said the club had made him what he was. He was one of those to whom the Missus had revealed the charm and graciousness, the intelligence and knowledge, the kindliness and helpfulness which sometimes makes her the greatest woman in the world. As, for so many, she often is.

K

Benny Caplan had, of course, learned his boxing at the club. He paid full tribute to its influence for good upon his early years, to his sense of sportsmanship, to his having become a better man.

David Jones said the club had given him many firm friends. Those friends were part of his life. It was a good point. Many had found companionship in the club.

The club had given me nothing. It had not changed my way of life. It had not made me anything I would not have otherwise become. For me, the Davenant Foundation School and such great teachers as J. R. Evans, who taught me to appreciate the beauties of the English language, had done for me what the Missus had done for brother Ben: exerted a formative influence on my character and career.

The club, I told them, had done nothing for me.

I don't think the Gaffer could ever forgive this. It was the denial of his life's work, a negation of everything he stood for, believed in: that the club made better men of *all* its members, every single one of them.

Of course the club had done nothing for me. But I had done nothing for the club, either.

Dave and Lily

OUT OF the sun shining and the wild wind gusting and the waves dancing and the world shaking itself in paroxysms of laughter . . . out of smiles and chuckles and devil-may-care unbridled, unqualified joy my sister Lily was born.

She was born to laugh her way through life and to bring laughter to the sad faces of those she met. She met nothing but agony and anguish most of the days of her life and she laughed her way through them.

She was young, always young; and jollity lit her span of living with incandescence. She radiated good humour. She exuded optimism. She was bathed in brightness. She saw only the sunkissed side of life.

She had the most wonderful sense of fun I have ever met. She wouldn't even be serious about the things she should have worried over.

From her earliest days she was a great mimic. The stage lost a fine comedienne in Lily. Brought up in a household where Yiddish and a sort of English were equally used, she had the gift of bilingual bastardisation we all inherited. And at school one day, when a little girl had upset the bag of coloured beads kids used to play with in those days, Lily complained to the teacher: "Sally Cohen shit out all my beads!" *Auschitten*, the Yiddish for to *spill*, was one of the words we threw into our daily speech. To shit out didn't mean for us what it meant to a horrified teacher who sent Lily straight to the Headmistress who heard my sister out and laughed heartily. Long years in the East End had taught Leah Titlebaum, that splendid Headmistress of the Jews' Free Girls' School whom many of my sister's generation remember with love and affection, that the King's English could be distorted by our kind of bilingualism.

Lily grew up a bonny girl. She took no prizes at school;

but had there been prizes for lovableness, she would surely have won a potful. Before the days when baby-sitting was an established profession, Lily baby-sat for all the inhabitants of the Buildings. She adored children.

She sat quite a lot for Abrams', the street bookmaker's wife. And one day he came storming to my mother's stall in Goolden Street and accused Lily of stealing money from the house. A fat little man he was, all mouth and gold teeth.

He " stood " in one of the three playgrounds of Broughton Buildings and people brought him bets. Look-out men, posted in the archway entrances, gave warning of an approaching policeman. Then all ran. Ten minutes later the group would re-form in one of the other playgrounds. Sometimes we wondered who ran faster: the nags or the bookies.

My mother was one of those foreigners who put the aitch in where it does not exist: there are many varieties of bastardised English spoken with a multitude of accents. You can tell the Spanish from the Italian from the French from the German. But the Polish accent is a little more bewildering, especially when it has been garnished with a soupçon of Russian and the lot transliterated into Yiddish. The Polish Pole drops the aitch when he speaks English. The Russian Pole, however, transposes it. And my mother was a great transposer of aitches.

" Ham Hi 'earing you correct, Mister Habrams. You ham saying that mine daughter Lily his stealing it from you maybe ha few shillings."

" A few flippin' quid more likely, Mrs. Alec "—addressing her, as was customary, by the Christian name of her husband.

" You hain't not using dirty language hin mine presence, Mister Habrams hor Hi'm sending for the policemen . . ."

" Sorry, Mrs. Alec. But your flipping daughter comes in to mind my flipping kid and then five flipping quid is missing and who the flipping hell pinched it but your flipping Lily-girl and I want my flipping money back or I'm the one what's gonna get the cops not you."

My Zaida was standing at the stall. There were but few words of English he understood and all of those were four-letter words. He listened to the oft-repeated four-letter-based gerund with growing consternation. Then he heard the word ' Lily ". Now she was his favourite daughter just as I was his favourite son. I suppose it was because we were the youngest.

My Zaida was a quiet soul. Except when he was roused. This man was throwing bad words at his daughter (my mother) and his granddaughter (Lily) too. Zaida felt passion stirring within him. Gently pushing my mother aside he faced the trucculent little bookmaker squarely.

He was no linguist, my Zaida, but his great gift of mimicry was one that his granddaughter, Lily, had obviously inherited. He stood in front of Abrams, feet astride. The two squat men faced one another, the red-faced, barrel-bellied bookmaker and my white bearded grandfather: Moses and Pharaoh.

I could tell Zaida was getting angry. His face was taking on the beetroot hue we all knew as a danger signal. It was a time to run. The bookmaker had been known to run well on other occasions. Now, foolishly, he stood his ground.

Zaida prompted him.

" Vot you say?"

" I say your flipping granddaughter Lily flipping well pinched some money from my flipping house. She's a flipping thief."

" You flipping thief." My grandfather's utterance of the unspeakable word was vehemently emphatic.

The bookmaker looked taken aback. But having begun a show he meant to see it through.

" Why you old bearded git. Fuckoff!"

" You fuckoff." Zaida was in his element. As long as you gave him words to repeat he would repeat them. The bookmaker played into his hands.

" Go back to Poland."

It was a curious thing that while my mother had been born in Poland and spoke Russian English, my grandfather, her father, had been born in Russia and spoke Polish English. Yet both had been born in the same place. The town, Brest Litovsk (or some such) was on the border and in the course of a generation had changed hands not a few times. My grandfather was staunchly anti-Pole. He remembered that the Poles had not been particularly fond of the Jews. Neither had the Russians; but Russian pogroms had generally been instigated by the military. The Poles, so my Zaida used to say, were all " bladden yiddified momsers ". They had been indiscriminately anti-Semitic. So the accusation, Pole, was just about the vilest insult you could throw at my grandfather.

He turned to the crowd which had assembled.

" See—he call me Polack. Me, Polack. Him English bastard. English momser bastard." That was tautologous. But the words on my grandfather's lips had a rolling sound.

" I show what I do."

He picked the rotund Abrams up by the waist and held him high above his head. Then, like the wrestlers he had seen back in the old country, Zaida began to twirl around with the now screaming bookmaker thrashing the air above his head.

I am sure he would have thrown him had not a bobby intervened.

At the sight of the law my Zaida put the man down. Abrams was sweating and shaking. My Zaida had a respect for policemen. I think they were the only people he was ever scared of. He had unhappy memories of the police forces of Russia and Poland in the bad old days and to him a pleaseman was a pleaseman. Under the impression that that was what one had to call them, he always addressed them as " Mister Please."

" Mister Please," he said, " dis man is bastard, momser bastard. I keel 'im stone dead mit vun Russian punch."

And, suiting action to words, he drew back his right arm till the fist touched his left shoulder and demonstrated the deadly blow, aimed outwards from the shoulder, that would chop the bookmaker down.

The constable knew my mother. All who knew her had tremendous respect for her. With a gesture of his arm he pacified Zaida and then asked my mother: " What's this all about, eh?"

My mother was not afraid of the law. She could lord it over minions. An inspector might inspire respect from her. But an ordinary policeman, never. Besides, wasn't this copper one of those to whom she regularly paid " shmear gelt "?

" Shmear gelt " was the money the stallholders slipped into the palms of certain policemen in Petticoat Lane every once or twice a week. Some of the men in blue strolled down The Lane with their hands out-thrust and the palms were automatically greased. You never even dreamed of not paying.

There were stories—such stories—of those who had tried not paying and had come to the market the next day only to find their pitches and stalls taken over by some unknown . . . stall-pigeons. If you had a stall in the market it was yours only by virtue of your co-operation with the law. So my mother paid this " shmear gelt " as everyone else in the market did. But at least she knew the constable. So did Abrams, if only to run at his approach.

She told him what had happened. " This man, 'e comes to mine stall hand 'e says that mine daughter, the youngest, Lily, what minds 'is baby sometimes, his taking money from 'is 'ouse. Now you know hofficer what ha honest family Hi 'ave. Hain't possible this should 'appen. When the great Rabbi Eleazar—you know it, the Talmud, officer?—was hasked to judge hif ha man were ha gunnof—ha tea leaf, hofficer—hor not, what was hit 'e said : ' Them what will judges be must first be judg-hed themselves and who wants to make . . . [there followed a string of erudite Hebrew, not market Yiddish] against ha man, must first 'imself proof beyond hall shadow of hinterference that . . . [and here followed another dazzling display of Talmudic philosophy]'"

My mother was now properly launched. She had her audience. It was standing four deep around the stall. And my mother was ten times the woman when there was an audience waiting to see how clever she was. She began to bowl them over.

" What his hit der Talmud says . . .?" Hebrew came pouring forth from her lips. She amazed the onlookers with words of learned length and thundering sound uttered in an ancient tongue. The policeman took off his helmet and wiped his brow. My Zaida stood by proudly, ten feet tall, that a woman, and his daughter, should show such deep knowledge of the wisdom of the rabbis and the sages. And Mr. Abrams was properly consternated. He didn't know whether he was coming or going. The whole affair was now over his head.

Eventually the policeman turned to him and asked : " Have you any proof?"

Abrams blustered. " Well, there she was, in my f . . .— excuse me, officer—in my house and the money was there and then we come back and it wasn't and if she didn't take it then all I can say is that the place is haunted and that it ain't,

Gawd knows, and she's got to 'ave the money around her somewhere or my name's not Solly Abrams."

"Your name," said the constable solemnly, "will be mud unless you can prove this. Do you want to make a charge?"

At this climatic stage in the proceedings a woman's voice was heard shrilling from a distance. We turned to look and there was Mrs. Abrams running towards us as fast as her fat little legs would carry her. She arrived at the stall breathless and thrust a purse into her husband's hands and gasped: "It . . . was . . . in . . . the drawer . . . all . . the . . . time."

My Zaida grasped what this meant before anyone else did, for suddenly he seized Abrams by the waist again, lifted the bookmaker over his head, and with one sweep of his arms flung him into a nearby dust cart where the fat little man settled gently down among the rotting garbage, the putrid fruit and the horse shit.

Then Zaida turned to the constable, shook him warmly by the hand, turned to the crowd and said: "You be it mine bankers for Polack," and walked away to recount the incident no doubt, to his friends in the Petticoat Lane parliament, the Thrawl Street pish-hooskie (the underground urinal where my Zaida and his cronies discussed affairs of great moment and set the world to rights). Bankers, vitnesses and voters were my Zaida's everlasting support. Once he had appealed to them he felt he could do no wrong.

The policeman blinked. Abrams hauled himself out of the muck. Mrs. Abrams began to sob hysterically. And the crowd started to laugh.

"Serves 'im bleeding well right," said the dustman.

"Flipping welsher," said his mate.

"Taken quids off me," said a woman, "and then thinks everyone's a big thieving bastard like hisself."

"Bloody tow-rag," said another.

The constable summed up the mood of the crowd in a trice. He put his hands in the small of Abrams' back and jostled him on.

"Now get on off," he said. "And don't let me catch you making any more trouble again."

My mother was grateful. "Come hon hin, constable," she said, "hand 'ave ha cup hof tea."

And he went. Everyone who ever began an argument with my mother ended up by taking tea in our house. House. Hark at me. Two rooms downstairs and a separate flat—O what sign of wealth—with another two rooms upstairs. And my Booba making tea. Endlessly.

My sister Lily was always a cause of some such trouble or other. She had such zest for life that it was inevitable she should come to stormier passes than those who amble their way through living. Most of the events that caught her in their swirl were tragic; yet she found fun in the oddest places and her laughter rings in my ears and will ring all the days of my life.

She was a gay one for the boys. She got involved—always innocently—with all the wrong kind. When she was sixteen and pretty good to look on, she had a married man of thirty-five fall in love with her. He was a musician, a sad-faced man. He fell in love with her laughter.

When the family frowned, she turned to me. I was always the one to whom she introduced her latest love and I was always the only one of the family the new boy-friend would meet.

She had no false respect for money. She worked as a typist when she left school and spent every penny she earned on cheap dresses and cheaper shoes. She was a flashy dresser. She lacked taste in clothes. She lacked taste in selection. But her heart was big. *She was the kindest soul that ever walked the face of the earth*. And because she was so open-hearted she could not understand why people, her family particularly, could not treat her with the same consideration as she would assuredly have treated them.

If she fell into debt she expected us, me especially, to help her. She expected it as a right because had positions been reversed, she would never have asked you why. She would just have given all she had.

My mother worried about her. My sister Betty loved her with a fierce love. My brother Mark shook his wise head over her: she was too wild for him. My brother Ben called her " Lul " and laughed with her. And I was her closest confidant and I joyed in her jollity and her warmness and her affection.

The affair with the musician looked to be going to end in

some tragedy. He was talking about leaving his wife with whom, it seemed, he had only one common interest: music. That had not been enough to keep a marriage going.

Then Dave appeared on the scene. He was a big, dark, semitically handsome lad. And he joyed in living, too. He had the body of a Greek god, teeth like shining pearls, crinkly hair as black as the raven's wing and a sense of fun that only somebody like Lily could hope to match.

They fell madly in love. And they laughed their way through all the days. They were the most in-love pair I ever knew. All the love poems ever written and all the love songs ever sung were meant for them.

Dave had no regular job and no regular money. But it was amazing how both managed without. They borrowed money to spend on pleasure. And always tried to pay it back. They lived for the day and they found something to laugh about in every second of it. Life was a lark.

They went on holiday to places I never even knew existed. They went away at week-ends. They went to the theatre and the cinema and to card parties. They ate out at restaurants. They bought lots of clothes.

They never stopped to think about the money they were spending. Money was nothing, happiness was all. How right they were.

My Booba didn't like the look of things. "A nogood-nicker," she called Dave; "an ohsverhf (a throw-out)". And the pair, "Shikey and Shemozzle" which I can only translate as "rack and ruin".

I don't think my brothers were all that keen on him either. But, as always, I stood by my younger sister's choice. Dave and I hit it off well. I liked his sense of fun. It was joyous and free. Laughter poured from the throat with the head flung back and the white teeth gleaming, bubbling like champagne.

He was a cousin of the then world heavyweight champion, though the Champ didn't know Dave existed; and he looked like the Champ, or at least he looked like the Champ looked in the American films and glossies. Dave was well over six feet tall, with an enormous chest, narrow waist, slender hips and big strong hands and feet. With a towel wound round his head he looked as if he had just come riding out of the desert to slay a few thousand infidels. Doovid Hamelech, I called him. David the King. And King he was—an Emperor among punier men.

What a swimmer he was, too. He practically lived in the water. We joined him in excursions to open air swimming pools. He was so magnificent in his bathing trunks that everyone turned their heads to look at him as he strode the bath or went swallow diving through the air.

He worked as a presser at the time. There is something about this pressing business I don't like. My father was killed by pressing. It is a tough job and the lifting of the heavy iron, and the steam, and the standing, affected my father's heart and he died. And Dave, it seemed to me, was another victim of the steam iron.

For he suddenly got pleurisy. And he went on swimming. And the pleurisy turned to tuberculosis and Dave began to cough blood. He was packed off to a sanatorium. Much against his will.

By this time he and Lily were man and wife, living from hand to mouth, with a baby on the way, no money in the bank, up to their ears in debt and quite the happiest couple I ever saw. They were passionately, madly in love. They were indeed twin souls, both scrupulously honest yet without sense of obligation, sense of responsibility or awareness of the future. Money had no meaning for them except as a means to buy not pleasure but joy. But their sense of honour and moral right was never in question. Yet—and it proves that one should not facilely measure any human being—they were a marvellous couple, devoted, full of fun, kind to the point of extravagance, and they loved the human race. Their honour rooted in consideration stood and faith ever faithful kept them staunchly true. And how intensely they loved life. How full of living they packed every hour.

So Dave was not one to stand the rigours of sanatorium life. He discharged himself. Lily was quite happy. They went on living their madcap life He changed his job. Became a furniture salesman. Bought himself a bicycle, getting me to sign my name to the hire-purchase contract, and chased around London. When he was not chasing sales he was shoving heavy furniture. He really did not worry about himself one jot. That was their great secret, their way of escape: they never worried for themselves, only for others.

Dave got worse. Thinner. Stooping. A second and then a third haemorrhage took him into hospital for long spells and out again before they could discharge him. And still the pair gadded about and kept late hours and filled the flat they lived in with card-playing friends and burned the candle at both ends and in the middle too.

The end was tragic. Dave began to walk with the aid of sticks. The magnificent figure of a man had become a shambles. And still the pair furiously refused to think of to-morrow. Maybe just as well. For there was to be no tomorrow. He was in hospital when he died. He called the nurse and before she could come to his side he died. He was twenty-eight, had barely begun to live, yet had crowded into that short hour of life more of tempestuous living than an entire generation of ordinary mortals. And he had been blessed with the kind of love that comes to few. This was the one everlasting light Lily could look back upon when it was all over, this tremendous love they had shared which had illuminated their lives. It was indeed a light that never lost its brilliance through all the passing, sad, unhappy years.

For after David she had a succession of tragic loves. An unhappy marriage with an old man who cared for her, I think, more than she cared for him. She left him.

There were others. She was chasing the shadow of Dave in other men and never finding it. Then, finally, marriage with a Scot of about her own age, a stolid, honest, respectable man who adored her. She liked him a lot too. No one could ever be like Dave again; but Stirling was a good man.

Then she grew ill. She had been ill many times over the years but, true to herself, shrugged off the operations and the treatments as if they were not worthy of her regard. One of her operations had been quite a serious one. She treated the whole thing as a joke. Surely Dave's spirit still haunted her. But this time the onset of the illness was insidious. She disregarded the symptoms. She had colitis and was told to go into hospital and get it treated. That was a laugh.

Towards the end she needed money badly. She tried to borrow from some rich friends and was refused. No one really thought she was serious. Real trouble she had always kept to herself—so she *couldn't* be in trouble.

But this time she was more than just deeply in debt. She

had the threat of a prosecution for non-payment of a debt incurred by a friend—a debt she had guaranteed to pay—hanging over her. This time, for the first and perhaps the only time of her life, she worried. And colitis it seems thrives on worry. It flared up. They got her into hospital. I saw her one Sunday looking well enough. About a week later I saw her again, her face shrivelled and screwed into the pillow, her teeth showing over her lip like a wild horse's, her figure shrunken and deformed. My sister, Polly, seeing her, screamed: " That's not my Lily, that's my Booba." She looked in early death as my grandmother had looked in the late, late years of her toilworn life.

So she joined her Dave. One hopes that, even if one cannot truly believe. But she believed. She believed with overwhelming faith she would see her Dave again.

And she died, believing.

And my heart broke. I thought to myself: Why should this happen to her of all people? Why is it the good who die young? Why Dave? Why Lily? She was my sister and I loved her. She had been really worried that time. She was afraid. And she had never been afraid in all her born days. But who ever dreamed that someone so alive could ever fail to laugh away any kind of trouble? Now, this minute, this day, tomorrow, anytime I would pay the earth to have her here with me again, to hear her laughing her way through life, to have her surround me with her sense of fun, maybe to borrow from her some of that maddening irresponsibility. For we all can be too sane, too responsible. Life is too short for us to be too serious about it.

Yet Life, at the finish, let her down: that same life she had treated so casually, even irresponsibly. It was as if fate got even with her for scorning it.

She never lent anything. She gave. She always gave with warmth and understanding and never expected to be thanked. Her possessions were everybody's. She had inherited my mother's way of sharing her last crust of bread.

And I suppose she thought that if she made demands upon people it was her right to do so. If she had had a million she would have given all of it away in acts of selfless charity. She gave her love of life, her good humour, her overwhelming generosity, her heart and soul to everyone she met. There was nothing phony about Lily. She was always herself. And life let her down. That almost child-like faith she had in being and living, that fervent belief in everything turning out well in the end, ended.

She was also like my Zaida whom we both worshipped. He too had no sense of Time's transience. Just as he lived to pray she lived to laugh. And in both of them there was a depth of heart-feeling affection that had to burst forth in a sort of irresponsible good nature which made people love them.

Both of them lived for the day. Both were real. They were what they were without the slightest sign of façade. You could read their characters in ten minutes. They were not complex. They were both simple people, taking delight in the simple things. They reasoned with their own childishly limpid logic, uncomplicating all the deviousnesses which surround most of us and cutting through mazes to find a direct route. They walked the broad easy way through life. Not for them the twists and turns and back alley meanderings. Everything, but everything, had a clear uncluttered solution. Life was plain and easy.

For him God. For her Dave—and when Dave went, love of laughter survived and with it my Zaida's unshakeable faith in the world to come. She knew, she just knew, she and Dave would one day be together again.

Only the dark depths of night to remember her and to hear from afar the magic of her laughter.

After her funeral my brother Mark, with breaking voice, read a passage from the Songs of Solomon:

"As the lily among thorns, so is my love among the daughters . . ."

Lily among thorns.

When Dave died I was writing a series for a national Sunday newspaper and I wrote a tribute to him. I dedicated it to "the memory of David who lived hopefully and suffered courageously and died before his time". I wrote—

THEY LIVE THOUGH THEY HAVE DIED

He wrote me a little note saying how much he liked these articles of mine. Next day he was dead.

He was twenty-eight. He had lived but a day, had hardly begun to live, in fact . . . and now he was dead.

For ten years he had borne pain and discomfort and agony, and throughout he had smiled and made others smile, and brought a little happiness to a world sadly in need of it.

He never moaned. He never grumbled. He never railed at the fate which had dealt him such a rotten hand in this card game we call life. Uncomplainingly, courageously, beautifully he had lived, and quietly he had died.

Did I say he was dead? He still lives on. In the hearts and the minds of those who knew him he lives on even now, on earth.

Someone smiles and I see Dave smiling; someone cracks a joke, and it is Dave's joke; they play hot music and I see Dave grinning and swaying to the rhythm and the swing; I see a flash of white teeth, an eyebrow lift quizzically, hear a full-throated laugh, a popular tune being hummed, and I know Dave will never die in my mind nor in the hearts of the people with whom he came in contact.

For some day, ten, twenty years from now, someone will do something, some little thing, and it will be Dave's way of doing it, and Dave dead will be Dave alive, if not in self, then in semblance.

And his words, his thoughts, his gestures, will travel round the world finding resting-places in many, and even those who never knew him will carry something of him in their lives.

For the man dies, but mankind lives on; the poet perishes, but poetry continues to sing; the painter hangs up his brushes for the last time, but portraits remain to attract the eye; footsteps fade away on the long and never-ending road of time, but the road goes on and on . . . in heaven *and* on earth he will find his immortality, and the young man of twenty-eight will not have lived in vain.

But some day, somehow, these things shall not be. Young men will not die before they have begun to live; wars will not bring suffering and despair and death to millions; epidemics will not stifle little babies in their cradles; poverty will not engulf the multitude.

Some day, somehow, it is all going to be very different, and everyone shall have a fair and reasonable chance of a fair and happy life.

And when that day comes the death of a young man will plunge millions into mourning and the whole world shall stand in silence if a babe dies.

And those who are alive and have strength must fight on until life becomes worth living, not only for themselves, but for everyone everywhere, until the Daves of this world do not, any more, die before their time.

And this is a fight that is really worthwhile. And those who fight it will have unseen millions, living dead, fighting with them and spurring them on to grander, nobler deeds.

That bit about in ten or twenty years time was prophetic. For Dave and Lily's son is the image of his father, the same man reborn. A little more sedate perhaps, a little less given to wild laughter, but in looks the same. And I never see him without seeing Dave or remembering Lily.

Dave had his tribute. And this has been Lily's. Now she is at sleep with yesterday's seven thousand years. I could not weep when she died. I was numb. Now I can weep for her.

If my tears be unavailing let my heart a chalice be.

SCHOOLDAYS FOR me were days of wonder and glory.

Maybe I was an early developer. I went to the Davenant Foundation School in the Whitechapel Road on a scholarship. I was a bright child with a retentive memory, especially for language. But a teacher at the school took this talent and shaped it. J. R. Evans, known to the boys as Gobby, because of the way he spat through his false teeth, was one of those Welshmen whose innate love of music shows itself in a worship of the beauties of the English language. Gobby discovered my love for words and nursed it and nourished it, even cherished it, so that I was able to find in English poetry the rainbow's end I had always looked for, the beauty that my imagination sought in out-of-the-way places, the love for the haunting cadence and the rhythmic phrase and the shining gem and the enchanting imagery. Together we trod the woodlands wild and heard again sweet wondrous sounds blown on notes of haunting gossamer through elfin reeds.

He and I were twin souls nursing the same secret passion: a love of words that made music, of syllables that sang, of sentences that danced.

He took me by stages from simple poetry to Browning and Joyce and Gertrude Stein and Proust. From Chaucer to Chesterton, from Wyclif to Wilde and Whitman, from Langland to Sinclair Lewis and Louis Untermeyer.

We ranged the field of the written word together, making serendipitous finds of words, couplets, odes, epics that even he had not before encountered.

He encouraged me at every step of the way and spurred me to write verse myself.

I had a working knowledge by then of French, German, Spanish and Italian and could read my way through poets in those languages. Davenant taught only French and Latin. But the languages master, Banks, gave me private study in Spanish

L

and Italian, and the Science master, Rivkin, gave me German lessons.

It was that kind of school. Dedicated. Where they found an apt pupil the teaching staff went out of its way to bring out his latent possibilities. Someone discovered I had a flair for languages and members of the teaching staff came to me with offers of assistance.

Like poetry I revelled in foreign sounds. They, too, were music for my ears.

My last year at school came all too soon. I was eighteen and destined for university. I had an Oxford scholarship. The school awarded me its School Leaving Scholarship. O, but I was going to be a great man. I was going to set the world on fire.

I wonder what happened to me along the way.

Two poems had made a terrific impact on my then immature, sensitive soul. One was in German, by Heine; the other in Spanish by Enrique de Mesa. They so fascinated me, the former by its simple declaration of love; the latter by its eeriness, that I set about translating them. Into poetry.

Gobby was so thrilled by the results that he sent for the masters who had guided me in German and Spanish and they, too, shared his delight.

The poem by Heine ran:

> *Wenn ich in deine Augen seh,*
> *So schwindet all mein Leid und Weh;*
> *Doch wen ich küsse deinen Mund,*
> *So werd ich ganz und gar gesund;*
> *Wenn ich mich lehn' an deine Brust,*
> *Kommt über mich wie Himmelslust;*
> *Doch wenn du sprichst " Ich liebe dich "—*
> *So muss ich weinen bitterlich*

Enthralled by its beauty, in love with love and loveliness, I found the English words coming almost unbidden. I had written:

> When, dear, I gaze into your eyes,
> My pain is gone, my worry flies;
> And when I kiss your lovely lips
> Life trembles at my fingertips.

I lay my head upon your breast
And Heaven is, with me, at rest.
Yet when you say that you love me—
Why must I weep so bitterly?

At eighteen years of age I reckon I did well enough. I have lived with the original and the translation for many years now and I would not want to change the latter. I could make it more adult, more sophisticated, more erudite. But Heine's poem has such startling simplicity, such resonant beauty of phrasing that I believe one should only attempt to transpose it into English poetry when one is young and all things are beautiful. After that, the world loses its essential quality to thrill, the ugliness seeps into one's soul and beauty no longer comes unbidden, in a torrent of words that set themselves down on paper and speak in the limpid language that measures the depth of one's own thoughts at that age.

There it was. A poem by Heine. Audaciously parroted by me in English. And they liked it. They loved it. Banks, Rivkin, Evans.

Between Spanish and Italian I found choice easy. Contrary to general uninformed opinion and much to the delight of Mr. Banks who was giving up spare time to teach me, I opted for Spanish as the lovelier language.

Italian is too prissy, too monotonous of word ending. Its many synonyms for " you " are fawning, obsequious and confusing. Its pretty sound lacks depth. The language has lost strength to its speakers and, without the firm hand of an Academy to keep it on the narrow path of orthodoxy, has run riot and become debased. Its euphony is specious and there is no grandeur, no majesty, no fire in its belly. It simpers where Spanish sings. It had given rise to no volume of great poetry, despite Dante and D'Annunzio and others. Opera is its voice and trite phrases and commonplace expressions are given over-emphasis by music which invariably outshines the speech it rounds, and makes sound appear greater than it is.

Italian has become the language of the streets. Anything goes. The apostrophe between apocopated words can or need not be used. Elision is a thing of fancy not of rule. A man can be called " *La* " and the intrusive " *ci* " occurs everywhere. Its plural endings are nowhere near as refined as the soft " *s* " in Spanish. Its possessive pronouns lack the simplicity of the Spanish " *su* ". And its infinite variety of pronouns drowns the language in a flood of irrationality, with " *li*," " *le*," " *lei*," " *Lei*," " *Loro*," " *loro*," " *gli*," " *glie*," *lo*, *la*, *La* and others fighting for understanding, so that even the Italians themselves do not know how to address one another. The newspapers call their readers " *voi* " but most others when addressing a crowd call them " *Loro* "; and I once heard an orchestra leader, talking to his musicians, begin by calling them " *Loro* " and end by calling them " *voi* ".

Lack of conformity, of uniformity, has debased the language into a pleasant sounding apology of a tongue; a vehicle for singers. The Spanish lisped " *c* " and " *z* " are far more delicately tuned than the ugly Italian " *dz* " or " *tz* " sound for " *z* ", the harsh " *ch* " for " *c* ". Italian may be facile but it is not felicitous.

The rigidity of Spanish has kept it truer to the Latin than the language that was founded in the ruins of Rome.

English is a flexible language, a growing, a living tongue; but colloquialisms and slang have to earn their way into English and are taken reluctantly into the Oxford Dictionary. The language lives and grows but is very discriminating in its choice; whereas, in Italian, the language, like Topsy, just grows. Without constraint or constriction it has become the most jumbled, tumbled, topsy turvy tongue in Europe.

Its pretences are ridiculous and its apparent euphony a trap to make the unwary and the surface-skimmers hail it as a thing of beauty. But it has no truth. It is all sham and confusion. Its beauty is shallow: its depths turbulent and muddied.

After all that I will sound unconvincing if I say I liked it. But I did. I liked all foreign languages. Though none as much as Spanish.

Spanish has the emotive depth I craved. Italian goes in light and froth while Spanish walks in mystery. Italian is a minuette, a gay scherzo, while Spanish is the dark lady of the sonnets. Italian is pastel. Spanish a blaze of colour. Italian is all classical but Spanish clicks its castanets and stamps its feet, and whirls in a riot of passion. Italian is artificial gardens full of artificial cherubs, over-life-sized. Spanish is fierce sunlight and dark shadow.

So I came to the poem by Enrique de Mesa and was overcome by its air of sombre foreboding. The underlying mystery of it sent a chill through my bones.

> *Ayer noche vino el lobo:*
> *Un zagal dice que oyó*
> *un aullido a medianoche*
> *que le helara de pavor.*
> *!Está loco el zagalillo!*
> *No hay en la sierra un pastor*
> *a quien le falta un cordero.*
> *— Es, sin duda, que soñó.*
> *A medianoche en la aldea*
> *una mozuela murió:*
> *secó la muerte el capullo*
> *de su tierno corazón.*
> *Ayer noche vino el lobo.*
> *Un zagal dice que oyó*
> *un aullido a medianoche*
> *que le helara de pavor.*

The nightmarish menace of the poem stirred the depths of my imagination. I could feel the black terror of the dark, the haunting fear of the atmosphere, the unquiet sense of an underlying, impending doom. The boy hearing the scream. They said it was a wolf. And then the mysterious death of the young girl. And the unanswered question: was it a wolf?

The heavy, slow syllables worked with passion to a dread climax. I *had* to translate and give it metre and scansion and rhyme.

I wrote:

> There was a wolf last night.
> A boy says he rose
> to hear a howl that froze
> his blood in fright.
> There was a wolf last night.
> Was the boy right?
> Terror begets error.
> From hillsides cold
> no shepherd from the fold
> a missing lamb has told.
> A howl? A scream?

Only a dream, a dream.
Yet at midnight, silence-laden,
in the village died a maiden.
Young bud withered on the bough,
no enchanted blossom now.
There was a wolf last night.
A boy has told
he heard a midnight howl
that made his blood run cold.

Mr. Banks, Mr. Rivkin and Mr. Evans expressed their appreciation, conferred in whispers, took the poems and sent me away.

Three weeks later they came upon me where I sat in a Latin class and took me by the hand and almost danced a jig round me, much to the amazement of the class and the utter dismay of the Latin (who was also the history) teacher. Then they read a letter aloud to the class. It was from one of the leading highbrow magazines of the day.

Both my poems had been accepted.

Even the Latin master shook my hand. The boys cheered. I had achieved print, good print, highly commended print, at the age of eighteen.

The poems duly appeared and I knew then that I wanted to be a writer. Nothing on earth would shake me from that resolve.

It was like wishing for starvation. Mother wanted me to be a doctor. Zaida wanted me to be a rabbi. And I wanted to be a writer and never have two pennies to scratch myself with.

Some years later I began to write. My books did well enough. But the East End was not in fashion. A few years after that, when I had ceased to write about the East End, it suddenly became fashionable again and a number of writers succeeded in achieving the fame and money I never did.

Browning said it plainly:

Hobbs hints blue straight he turtle eats.
Nobbs prints blue—claret crowns his cup.
Nokes outdares Stokes in azure feats. Both gorge.
Who fished the murex up?
What porridge had John Keats?

The Murex is a purple dye which, to get, Tyrrhenian fisher-men spent a lifetime clawing from the sea. Those who used the dye, those who imitated its rich purple in various shades of blue—the Hobbs, the Nobbs, the Nokes, the Stokes—they grew wealthy while the poor fishermen starved. What Brown-ing is trying to say is that brilliance, such as Keats, goes un-rewarded, while the followers sup all the soup Keats never ate.

I am not trying to say that mine was brilliance. But it was original. The late James Agate recognised that. He called me " that original utterance ". But I never made it. Those who came after me did. Okay. So that's the way the cookie crumbles. You take it or you leave it. Lady Luck wasn't meant to ride alongside you. It's just one of those things.

But when, even after this, I again tried an East End book —*No Tears in Aldgate*—and the reviewer on *Punch* said I was copying the fashionable literary world of the East End, my cup of anger, disappointment and frustration ran over. I had been one of the beginners of the vogue and I was accused of copying. I had made no real money at it. Those who followed, had. Yet when I reverted to the scene that people I (and writers like Willie Goldman and Simon Blumen-feld) had wasted years of our life describing—to little financial benefit or purpose—I was accused of being an imitator. How it rankled. Be kinder to me this time, Joanna!

All this frustration and disappointment was a long way ahead of me yet. At the time I wanted desperately to be a writer. And even if I could have foreseen what a miserable reward writing would bring, I should still have elected to write. As well tell the heart to stop beating. This is the way I was, am. My blood drips red, writes blue and dries black. I am an incurable sufferer from a dreaded disease, *cacoethes scribendi*, the itch, the writing itch. I scratched then, an eigh-teen-year-old, and my dearly beloved Gobby Evans encour-aged me and made me live with the dream.

But there were no colleges of writing. Where did one go to become a writer?

My last days at school were spent in looking forward eagerly to Oxford. On the last day I went round shaking hands and Gobby held my hand a long time and I thought to myself, Why doesn't the old josser let me go my rounds?

and I went away and I forgot the school that had shaped me, formed me, fashioned me, given me poetry to love and beauty to appreciate.

I never went back.

All my life this casual parting has haunted me. Gobby Evans did more for me than any man who ever lived. Banks, Rivkin and other teachers devoted themselves to the furtherance of my talents. And I shook their hands and said *Goodbye* and never went back.

Goodbye. *Arrivederci. Hasta la vista. Au revoir. Auf wiedersehen.* But Goodbye the most final. Farewell. Till I never see you again, *ave atque vale.* Till we meet a thousand years hence, till the mountains skip like rams and all the flowers of the field dance the polka. Till music flows from the skies like rain and the lion lies down with lamb and people everywhere love their neighbours as themselves and war is forgotten and death is outmoded and cancer is no more. Goodbye. Till the impossible happens. Till a dream comes true, goodbye. We shall never meet again on the bonny banks of Time. Farewell, a last farewell to all my promised greatness.

I shook their hands and said the irrevocable goodbye. And never went back.

Gobby, I hope you sleep soundly on some Welsh hillside. I shall never forget. I didn't thank you, but I shall never forget.

So I went on to Oxford. But because I knew no Greek I could only get a free place and it was impossible for me to stay there. Half-way through the first miserable term I decided to give it up and got myself transferred to London University. There, because I had the scholarships, I got the money.

No Greek was no bar to progress . . . at London.

At school I had always had friends. John Mather, the brilliant thinker and speaker; Roger Bagehot, the sex-mad lovable harum-scarum; Shorty, the six-footer, handsome and conceited. I was popular. I was good at games, good at my work. At Oxford I experienced real loneliness for the first time. I was a nonentity, a minnow among Tritons.

I was surrounded by a mass of public school boys speaking in their strange accents, formed into cliques by virtue of the schools they had been at together or by reason of the societies and clubs they joined that I could not afford. I was an alien, an outsider. My accent was unmistakably East End. I had nothing in common with them.

Things are different now, but in those days talent was not the key that opened the gates of Oxbridge. I have never, in one place, met so many young men without any real brain, without any real ability, without any thoughts beyond fleeting pleasures. They were shallow shells, apologies for the real young men I had known in the East End. They were men born with golden spoons in their mouths, unused to pain or hurt or disappointment unless it be the peevish disappointment of the spoilt child deprived of what it wants; they had never known suffering. They had no conception of what life could be like.

Outside the ancient, ivied walls hundreds of thousands of men were on the dole. Thousands marched on London. Poverty was everywhere. Children died of malnourishment. Young men like themselves stood in queues for a pittance or were subjected to degrading tests to determine whether they had any right to survival. And here they were, the favoured of the community, elegantly strolling their way through a life that had been made just for them. Nitwits, drips, brainless idiots, chinless wonders. Empty gasbags.

Of course there were exceptions. Talent is not the exclusive attribute of the lower classes. But more than three-quarters of the young men there had no right to be there. There were scholars in the East End who had more inherent ability and had worked harder at developing it than these favoured ones toiled at their rowing, cricket or rugger.

I went down, voluntarily, from Oxford. It was the end of a dream I had cherished since I was ten. Oxford had always been, for me, the rainbow's end. And when I got there I found it was impossible to survive on rainbow's colours. Something more solid was vital.

At the London colleges I grew even more amazed by the lack of ability that showed itself all over the lecture rooms and theatres. Here, apart from scholarship boys, were the second-raters: those with not quite enough money or breeding or pull or influence to make the Oxbridge grade but with good second class public school backgrounds, good enough for the lesser London University anyway. Talent-wise they were made to look fourth and fifth raters by the scholarship boys.

Maybe because there were proportionately far more boys from lower class homes at London than there had been at Oxford, maybe because the differences of class were more apparent—whatever the reason, the first intimation I ever had that anti-Semitism was a living reptile was at London University.

Hitler was just about making it at the time. Some people over here gloried in the power and ruthless evil of that way of life. At least, college seemed to be full of a Fascist clique and its supporters.

Students would sidle up to me and say, " Why do you keep company with those Jews?" meaning Aaron Leftbaum and Abram Abramovitch who travelled up and down with me each morning on my way to college.

Aaron and Abram were both brilliant students. You had to be brilliant if you wanted to get into London's favoured college and just happened to be Jewish too. There was no obvious bar but there were some very sinister ones.

When I would turn upon my enquirers and tell them I was Jewish too, they'd look at me as if I had taken leave of my senses and splutter: "But you play football and cricket!" implying that it was physically, mentally and psychologically impossible to be a Jew and play games too.

Fan me with a lollipop, Brother, knock me down with a fart. It was the strangest thing since salted peanuts. A Jew who played games. How incredible can you get?

What use was it trying to point out to them the host of Jews who had made their mark in British sport? Without mentioning a single boxer I could have named three of England's amateur soccer eleven, including my own brother; Britain and Europe's leading fencer; Britain's champion gymnast. And at least two County cricketers I knew. But both had changed their names. As had the Soccer pros. who would otherwise have needed police protection.

What use is argument against those who won't hear?

Even my own kind were wrath with me, and have been all these years, because I separate " us " from " them ". They hate it. The bigger they are, the more famous they are, the more British they are, the more they hate it. One well known

Jewish actor nearly came to blows with me because, as he insisted, I kept on separating "us" from "them" or, in effect, "him" from all those he wanted to be part of.

As I've said before and will go on saying: it's no use. We will never be accepted. Henriques, Cohen, Levy, Sassoon or Rothschild can be kings in their own right but under a Hitler they will always be Jews.

It can't happen here? It nearly did in the thirties. One day I came into the shower to find a gang of thugs beating Aaron Leftbaum and Abram Abramovitch with gym slippers while they kept them under the freezing cold douches. I rushed in and was set upon by the gang. Aaron and Abram, though they were no fighters, rushed to join me and a wild scrap took place on the wet tessellated floor of the shower bath. A scrap in which we were worsted. And bruised.

The next day the Senior Tutor sent for me.

Trouble.

I had been reported for creating a disturbance. It was implied that Jews were always a source of trouble. They weren't even good scholars, just quick to absorb surface information without ever having real profound knowledge of their subject.

He was a short, tubby man, with a Vandyke beard, very public school and Oxbridge, very correct. He swept his gown round him as he walked, his two feet almost scraping one another as they passed in walking, the measured tread giving him a strange grace and nobility.

He was so sincere in his talking, eyeing me with grey eyes that breathed conviction, that he almost had me believing in his rubbish about Jews being poor scholars, really; just quick on the uptake.

However, when he was saying that Aaron and Abram, my not so well chosen friends, were not even the good scholars they had pretended to be and that I, because of my name, was not even the non-Jew I had pretended to be, I suddenly lost my temper.

"Bloody fascist!" I said.

His grey eyes blazed. He rose, swirling his gown around him, in an effeminate gesture.

"What was that you said?"

"I called you a bloody fascist. You've been preaching

Hitlerism to me and I've only just recognised it."

" How dare you talk to me like that!" He was all out-raged dignity and quivering beard.

" How dare you talk to *me* like that," I replied.

Even as I faced him, determined to stand my ground this once, I realised that I might be throwing away all I had ever worked for: that this fierce-looking man who so resembled the popular portrayal of a Hun might have me expelled.

He stood up and pointed a finger at me with a gesture so dramatic that it could have come out of a film director's cue to his cameraman. *Shoot!* it said.

I didn't wait. I plunged in.

" Do you know what happened? Do you really know? Do you know that some of your public school gangsters pushed Leftbaum and Abramovitch under the showers and kept them there under the freezing cold water by hitting at them with slippers? That all I did was what any decent chap would do —went to their rescue? And you give me all this drivel about Jews making trouble and being sham scholars and a lot of bilge like that. Have you forgotten Disraeli? And Einstein? And Herbert Samuel? And the man who gave this col-lege the money to build this wing, this room we are now in?"

At the mention of the benefactor, the Senior Tutor dropped the accusing finger and sat down and began to wave his hand airily as if dismissing me.

I turned. At the door he cautioned: " No more trouble, now."

" I won't go looking for it," I said, " but if it finds me I'll not run away."

The next day, when the college eleven went up on the board my name was not in it. For the first time, I had been dropped.

I had the unusual distinction of playing inside-left for the University and opening its batting without being a member of my college teams.

That same year I was the only Jew who passed. Six others, all the rest in fact, including Leftbaum and Abramovitch, were sent down. A good case could doubtless have been made out for their failure. Yesterday it was Cohen. Today it's d'Oliviera. Maybe we were too involved to see the truth.

I hope the Senior Tutor rests easily in his grave. He lived to the grand old age of 97 and died surrounded by academic honours and awards. But for me his honour rooted in dishonour stood. I was sorry when he died for the way he had lived.

So, at the tender age of twenty, I grew confused. I had always thought rather contemptuously of that large slice of the working class which spent its wages on beer and gambling and kept its families short of necessities. I had always looked upon the pub with disfavour. I had called it the invention of the upper classes to keep the lower classes happily in their place. I had no patience with those of the working class who were content to remain stupid and ignorant. The fish and chips mentality. But now I found the so-called upper classes nothing to write home about. They were just as stupid, but educated-stupid; just as intolerant, but nice-mannered intolerant; just as happy with their sozzle, only for them it was spirits.

I began to get a feeling that people everywhere were basically evil. I no longer believe this. I haven't believed it for many years. But then, in my eighteenth year I began to think it and it made me sad. It was a rotten, rotten, rotten, rotten world.

In a way I had been protected. I had had dealings with people, mostly Jews, who spoke one's own language of behaviour, who thought along one's own lines of environmental reasoning and logic; who accepted you as you accepted them, with all their individual differences, as people like yourself. There had never been any pronounced clash of human being versus human being in my East End. Polacks v. Choots, Jews v. Gentiles, Catholics v. Protestants, drinkers v. non-drinkers, barrow boys v. stall holders—all these had been games. Now I experienced bloody war.

Suddenly, for the first time, I sensed the bitterness in racial discrimination, religious discrimination, working-class discrimination, left-handed discrimination—once it began, where did it leave off?

I saw the wickedness to which apparently ordinary men could be driven by the inferiority instincts which led them to class others as inferior.

In college I saw thugs beating two harmless, pleasant, shy,

retiring, modest, diffident Jews who would never have harmed a soul. And, because I interfered, I was tarred with the brush that sears, castigates and crucifies.

Seventeen had been a very good year. Eighteen was a stinking year.

I think I began to realise then what I had enjoyed at school and to miss it for the first time. But by then it was too late. The moving finger had written on and all my wishing would not lure it back to cancel half a line.

It was then, too, I realised the inevitability of gradualness, not as a political conception, but as a living conception. Time that's lost, we had sung at school, may all retrieve. Balls. Time that's lost is down the drain, fini, caput, gone, gone, gone. The scientists say nothing is ever destroyed. I don't know about that. All I know is that a hell of a lot is lost. And once it goes you can never get it back. Never.

I HAD been writing since I was knee high to my mother's Edwardian skirts. Like Pope I lisped in numbers for the numbers came. As I grew up I read obsessively, consuming the printed word like a prairie fire consumes whatever stands in its way. What with reading and writing I became, at sixteen, seventeen, and eighteen, when I first began to write with an eye to publication, a parody of all the great writers I had met.

I was a succinct, powerful Hemingway; a wild, participle-prone Saroyan; a lush, image-drenched Thomas Wolfe looking-homeward angelically; a terse, fulsome Fitzgerald; a casual, debonair Maugham. I was a parody not only of others but of myself.

The East End boy, searching for beauty, striving to find the secret of living in a grey world, I yearned for what I knew not. I was in love with love, physically, morally and mentally; a part of all that I met, totally involved in people and their lives and their day to day struggle for existence.

Poetry wrapped me in dreams. Word music haunted me, enchanted me. The violin made me cry. I was near to tears when petals fell. Death saddened me. Old age grieved me. Suffering angered me. Over sensitive, a dreamer in dust, I found in writing the realisation of all my ideals, the relief from all my tensions.

My friends were complementary to me. In their company I found the tougher virtues one needed to survive.

Shorty, the six footer, was handsome. His black curly hair, his finely chiselled face, his gay manner and his overweening conceit were a good foil to my more subdued personality. He was the egoist, *comme le chien*, while I was the egotist, *comme le chat*. He manifested his superiority in his walk, in his clothes, in his assertions of his own prowess while I nursed to myself my talent and my ability at the sports he fancied himself at.

But he was good fun. The girls loved him. And in his company one found oneself attracting girls one would never have been able to talk to if left to oneself.

Shorty was never as short of money as the rest of us. His parents owned a restaurant in Whitechapel Road and ran a car long before most people even dreamed of possessing one. Today he is a famous restaurateur. He left my world when we were leaving school, I to go to University, he to Polytechnic to learn about hotel management. Funny isn't it? You grow up with someone, you are so closely interknit, so dependent on one another for company, know so much about each other, spend hours in each other's houses, days in each other's company, exchange points of view, secret thoughts, discuss ambitions, reveal yourselves to one another, are like David and Jonathan—and then, circumstances part you, and it's as if you never knew one another.

The moment we left school we lost touch. I have seen him only twice in over twenty-five years. Both were accidental meetings and both of us were uncomfortable in each other's presence.

What happens to people to make them drift apart like this?

Little Harry was different. He was sharp, shrewd, quick—especially at mathematics; but he lacked imagination. He was a practical soul, cheery, bright, perky as a sparrow. His people manufactured underwear. He became a director of the firm which later was merged with a world-famous underwear manufacturing house and Harry became a millionaire. He was never as close to us as we, without him, were amongst ourselves—if you understand me. He joined our little group and found pleasure in our company, but we never missed him when he wasn't there. We would ask each other *Where's Shorty, John, Roger?* but never *Where's Harry?*

Harry became a millionaire. His picture was in all the papers. He was thirty-five. At thirty-seven he had a coronary and died. What good were his millions?

Roger Bagehot was the life and soul of the party, the oldest and most experienced. He knew Life. He was completely without fear, possibly because he was completely without moral or spiritual guilt. Sex-mad, viewing every girl he saw as a potential bedmate, he made life for our clique exciting and rumbustious. An awkwardly built tousle-headed clown of a fellow, Roger just could not be serious. He tumbled dozens of girls into bed and laughed at himself as much as he laughed at life.

He was laughing, they tell me, when the mortar bomb blew him up just as his company crossed the Rhine. He had just finished telling a funny story. And Roger always laughed heartily at his own jokes.

John Mather was the enigma of the clique. He was a thin, fair boy with a clipped way of speaking. We all knew he was bright, yet in class he used to finish way down near the bottom. Other boys wondered what we, the bright ones of the class, saw in this dullard.

He was a nervous, peculiar boy, given to sneering remarks and sudden, unaccountable flashes of temper.

Harry once came into the classroom with a huge ice cream balanced on a cone and John swept it to the ground for no reason at all. Once we were playing table tennis in the Sixth Form Prefects' Room and John deliberately trod on the only ball.

I understand it all now. Then, of course, some of his actions merely roused resentment. It took me nearly forty years to know what made John Mather tick. And by then the tick was slow and faltering.

He was the son of a father who had died of tuberculosis. Not only his father but his father's seven brothers had all died of tuberculosis. John's younger brother had already contracted it when John was about fourteen. John lived in the shadow of this illness and knew, positively knew, that one day he would succumb. He was extremely poor, underfed I guess, and malnourished. His mother worked like a slave to try and keep her two boys alive.

It is easy to see now how the longing for all the good things others had, had built up in John the strange spites and jealousies he suffered from as an adolescent. He even envied me my home, my sisters, my brothers, my way of life, though he loved them in his own way.

He spent a great deal of time in our house. My mother liked him enormously. She was sorry for him. She mothered him, giving him more affection than she gave her own sons, feed-

M

ing him every five minutes, even giving him pocket money.
John liked our family. He had a secret pash on one of my
sisters and welcomed the chance to visit us. "Where shall we
go?" I'd ask. "Let's go to your place," he would say. Always.
And there he'd spend the whole day as an accepted member
of the family.

Suddenly, when he was in his sixteenth year and a few
months away from his matriculation examination, he fell sick
with pleurisy.

When they X-rayed him they found tuberculosis. Active. It
was the inevitable death blow which he had always feared and
which, always at the back of his mind, had made him seem
different from ordinary boys. He was, for example, a very
aggressive youngster, always putting his fists up and showing
eagerness for fight; it was his way of proving to himself that
he might look a weed but could be tough. He played cricket
and football with us, very badly, but determined it seemed
to prove himself as good as any. He ran in the school athletics
championship, scorning the sprints, to prove to himself and
others over a mile and more that he was as fit as they. He
fought the disease, consciously or unconsciously, every step
of the way, with every ruse he knew. But it wouldn't be staved
off.

He went into Brompton Hospital first; then into a sanatorium. Shorty, Roger, Harry and I all missed him. We wrote
to him and had one or two letters back. But, truth to tell, he
was soon forgotten. The coming examination was on our
minds. Boys in other schools might get a general certificate
pass, but Jewish boys at Davenant always got matric. To get
anything less was considered failure.

They talk glibly today about higher standards of education.
Higher? I don't know about that. Today a G.C.E. pass is the
accepted standard. In our day that was valueless. It had to be
nothing short of matric. Today's O-level was yesterday's
failure. O-level is fairer, certainly. Today the youngster who
has one weak subject can get round it. In our day the student,
before being accepted at a university or, for that matter, as a
sixth former, had to pass in English, Maths, one foreign language, either physics or chemistry, and either history or geo-
graphy. He had to get five passes to matriculation standard—
about twenty per cent above the then school-leaving certifi-

cate standard—to reach the sixth form. He *had* to pass in English, Maths and a foreign language.

Innumerable bright boys never got into the sixth. Some stumbled over maths and could never make it. Others found the foreign language the insuperable difficulty. When I reached University I was furious when I thought of the fine minds who had failed to make the grade because one subject always beat them; yet there, at Oxford, and at London too, the place was filled with nitwits who had bought tutors and taken a ridiculously easy entrance examination to a college of the university and paid for their place. While many East End young men I knew, with good brains and real ability, had failed to get matric and had had to sacrifice a scholastic career and an entire future because they were no good at one subject, one obligatory subject. There must have been many promising doctors, teachers, lawyers, dentists, civil servants and priests and rabbis lost to the nation then because they had one subject they could never master.

Yet they talk so easily today about higher standards of education. Ours were not only high, they were formidable.

John was not expected to pass to matriculation standard before he got ill. And since he was sick no one even expected him to take the examination.

But they reckoned without that terrific inner toughness. John was allowed to come back for a fortnight and sit the examination. When the results were made known we refused to believe them.

He had taken eight subjects and won eight distinctions. I, the school's most promising pupil until then, had five distinctions. Shorty four. Harry three, the minimum for a " pass with honours ". Roger failed. He got the equivalent of seven O-levels but he failed because he failed to reach matriculation standard in French. Imagine that today: seven O-level passes regarded as failure!

But John, the weak, the despised, the frail, the sick John had scored eight out of eight—all distinctions. Without attending a single class, without taking a solitary note, without being taught, without guidance, he had scored a perfect result. He had sat in his bed there in the sanatorium and read and worked and done it all alone.

He went back to the sanatorium but, after a month or two,

was allowed to leave. He rejoined us in the sixth. He was instantly made a House Captain. I was School Captain and it was my task to allocate the large playground for after-school House football practice. Each House had use of the playground in turn. The school elevens had them on the fifth evening. It was accepted that all Captains of other Houses could play every night, if they so wished. Shorty and I so wished. We played football with all the other Houses and their captains played with our Houses when they felt like it. If you were keen on games you could, therefore, play every evening of the school week.

The first week John was back Shorty and I arrived in the playground on John's House playground session, all ready for action. John refused to let us play. It was his House evening and nobody, but nobody else could join in. We tried arguing. But John could be fiercely obstinate. We did not play that night and Shorty never forgave John the insult.

He was changed. Not only had the long illness brought to the fore an inner brilliance nobody knew he had, but it had also brought about remarkable changes in his character. He was now strong and masterful, almost dictatorial in his attitude. He resented being told what to do. He was more aggressive than he had ever been but the nature of his aggression was also changed: it was now an obstinacy of mind, and I have no doubt of spirit too; a fierce pride in his power of argument, not merely the truculent gestures of a child.

He suddenly blossomed into a brilliant debater. He could speak *ad lib*, on any subject and go on speaking intelligently, making telling points, throwing in the odd quip, showing a force and fury uncommon in schoolboys.

He could argue—about anything—long and passionately, with inspired logic and almost professorial reasoning.

He showed signs of becoming a martinet in his dealings with the younger boys. The conceit that I wore close to my heart and Shorty on his sleeve, showed up in him in ever facet of his being. He walked slowly and firmly, pacing the ground with measured, deliberate, masterful tread. He held himself upright, fighting perhaps against the stoop engendered by a weak chest. His voice had the throaty timbre of tuberculosis sufferers: in him it produced a richness of voice quality rare in seventeen year olds.

Shorty and I continued to be friends with him. Harry and Roger could not stand him; he made them feel so inferior. The school disliked him—and he knew he was unpopular. But he didn't care. Shorty and I fought to be popular. We couldn't have stood it if we had thought we weren't liked. John didn't care. Everyone called him a bastard. Except my mother. She doted on him. Now that he was clever too, she worshipped him. She adored clever people.

John went on to take Higher Schools, the equivalent of to-day's A-level examination. He took four subjects and got four distinctions. He was awarded a State Scholarship, a rare award then for an East End boy. No more than twenty were given in the entire country.

He went to the London School of Economics and became a leading light in the debating society. He took a First in Economics. Then, unable to decide what he wanted to do, went on to King's College and took a First in English and History. He could do almost anything in the scholastic field. He had become a genius.

Hannan Swaffer heard him speak one night and was very impressed. Swaff turned John's thoughts towards journalism.

John became a feature writer with the *Daily Mirror*. He began to write a London-after-dark type column. It meant going to night clubs and living the gay life and drinking hard and gleaning gossip.

I saw him occasionally. It was invariably during the evening when his work session began. He wore immaculate evening dress, always sported a white carnation; had grown a little ginger beard to make him look older, more distinguished. He appeared to be curt, but his speech had been clipped even more than was natural to him, so that he spat out syllables like pips; and every so often one of the pips exploded. He was never short of feminine company, the kind of debbish company I could only dream of meeting and with which I should have been ill at ease anyway.

He drank. He drank a lot.

Hugh Cudlipp relates in *Publish And Be Damned* how he had to fire John because John had upset someone with one of his over-spiced paragraphs.

John was apparently on contract; and when he heard the sound of the signing-off fee he was going to get, he was overjoyed. It was one of the early golden handshakes. John was in the money. For the first time in his life he had capital.

He went on to found a weekly news magazine and then went to *Reynolds News* as Art Editor. I met him there. I was writing football for them at the time and he tried to help me all he knew. He was abrupt, he could say things like: " I'm busy, can't you see? And I have my own job to worry about without having to worry about yours." And he did say just that to me, once. But when I came to face the situation which had arisen which had given me cause to worry—some question of my losing the free-lance job to a staff man—there was no situation. He had erased it.

The next time I ran across him was when I sold the first ever short story the *Daily Express* published after the war. It was in the Press Club at about six o'clock one winter's evening. John had been there a long time. He was never the worse for drink but his red-rimmed eyes and his blown-up truculence, hard to take at the best of times, were evident.

When I told him that I was going across the road to see the Features Editor he told me he was on the *Daily Express* now. He was the chief re-write man. I didn't realise how important a job it was then. But when I talked to various staffmen I know that though they disliked John, they respected his brilliance. Everyone said what a great journalist he was.

When my short story was published the *Daily Express* had the nerve to send me eight guineas; when I complained bitterly about the smallness of the fee the Features Editor wrote me a letter telling me that I ought to be proud to have a story published in the *Express*.

John was furious when I told him what I had been paid. He marched into the Features Editor's office and began to let fly a flood of choice abusive words, the four letter ones fitting beautifully into a wonderful tirade of invective. It didn't do any good. The paper wouldn't look at another of my stories, didn't up their fee and even rejected ideas I sent them for further stories. But John felt good. He had shown me what a power he was in *Expressland*.

And he was a power. Journalists told me that he was a real bastard but when it came to words he had no master.

He did fabulously well at the *Express*. He was appointed Night Editor. When the Bannister four-minute mile was run,

John was on night duty and, though he knew sweet fanny adams about athletics, wrote a front-page story that is even now quoted as one of the finest ever written.

It was John who altered the appearance of the front page to take the lead story down its centre and who established a trend in journalistic layout that has become the general pattern.

He was earning big money; travelled widely; lived expensively. He never contacted me—we always met by chance; but he was reasonably friendly when we did meet. My mother, however, refused to forgive him because he never got in touch with her. She had done so much for him when he was in need. Now he did not remember her.

He had grown obese. He was a heavy drinker, heavy smoker, wild liver. He had married a woman journalist but his marriage went on the rocks after only a short while, and his wife took away their two daughters. I don't think John ever saw the children again.

Then, at the height of his power, at the summit of his brilliance, he had a coronary and was retired. With another fat golden handshake.

When his mother had died I had sent him a polite note. I never got a reply, and forgot the incident.

But, almost ten years later, I found a bulky envelope in my post and, on opening it, saw a green tattered autograph album fall on to the table. I took it up with trembling hands. It was the album I had filled with scribblings when I was eleven, twelve, thirteen, and John was my best friend, and the world was young.

And with it a sad note from John.

Suddenly the years fell away, all those wasted years of striving and non-fulfilment, all the anguish and the despair —Dave's death, Lily's, the war and its horrors—and everything was as it was when life burgeoned and there was blossom on every bough.

We were happy boys again, happy boys together. There were Shorty and John and I walking the London streets deep in philosophical discussion, putting the world to rights, pulsating with cold passion and the glory of being alive, revelling in each new day, each fresh experience.

A voice from the dead past, the always alive past, the forgotten past, the ever remembered past. My tattered little book of scribblings. There lay my youth. There I was, myself as a boy; all the words I then thought beautiful, beautiful still; quotations from my favourite poets, still my favourite quotations.

In the album such quotations as:

> Where but to think is to be full of sorrow
> And leaden-eyed despairs ...

> ... for many a time
> I have been half in love with easeful Death ...

> ... The blue
> Bared its eternal blossom, and the dew
> Of summer nights collected still to make
> The morning precious ...

> Where youth grows pale, and spectre-thin, and dies ...

Ah David, ah Paddy, ah Keats. Youth growing pale and spectre-thin. Keats, then in my youth, summing up for me all that I have since tried to say in oceans of words.

And more Keats, Keats my God of Poesie, even then:

> The silver, snarling trumpets ... the honey'd middle of the night ... her rich attire creeps rustling to the knees ... drowsed with the fume of poppies ... O aching time! O moments big as years! ... And then there crept A little noiseless noise among the leaves, Born of the very sigh that silence heaves ...

Keats. The little green album full of gems of syllables woven into shining words to make a garland of poetry.

And the last Keats quotation: *Here lies one whose name was writ on water*. On water? No. No and a thousand times No. In my heart. In many hearts forever.

Browning of course:

> The sin I impute to each frustrate ghost
> Is—the unlit lamp and the ungirt loin ...

> What so wild as words are? ...

> Then welcomes each rebuff
> That turns earth's smoothness rough ...

Lots of Browning.

Where the quiet-coloured end of evening smiles . . .

A mile of warm-scented beach . . .

Does he paint? He fain would write a poem—
Does he write? He fain would paint a picture . . .

Never the time and the place
And the loved one all together . . .

That low man seeks a little thing to do,
Sees it and does it:
This high man, with a great thing to pursue,
Dies ere he knows it . . .

A castle, precipice-encurled
In a gash of the wind-grieved Apennine . . .

Lots of Browning. Browning who was born when Keats was seventeen, who was nine when Keats died.

And Tennyson, mostly In Memoriam, the greatest poem in the English language:

But, for the unquiet heart and brain,
A use in measured language lies;
The sad mechanic exercise,
Like dull narcotics, numbing pain . . .

The last red leaf is whirl'd away . . .

I do but sing because I must,
And pipe but as the linnets sing . . .

Now fades the last long streak of snow,
Now burgeons every maze of quick
About the flowering squares and thick
By ashen roots the violets grow . . .

There, where the long street roars, hath been
The stillness of the central sea . . .

Tennyson. To whom Gobby Evans introduced me many years before my time. The entire album a tribute, a memorial to Gobby. For the quotations with which it is littered are the gems he made me recognise, first with my eyes and then with my ears and then with all my heart. And his spirit breathes through the schoolboy hand and the immature writing.

The book is full of Shakespeare, with many additions neatly printed in John's hand. Swinburne, the Rosettis, the Bible, Ovid, Horace and Cicero, even a trite verse from a calendar—

> It's easy enough to be pleasant
> When life flows along like a song
> But the man worth while
> Is the one who can smile
> When everything goes dead wrong.

And, my favourite then, and still one of my favourites I think, the quatrain by James Russel Lowell that pays tribute to the music that my poetic friend, Fitzgerald, found in Omar Khayyàm:

> These pearls of thought in Persian gulfs were bred,
> Each softly lucent as a rounded moon;
> The diver Omar plucked them from their bed,
> Fitzgerald strung them on an English thread.

The book is a shipload of memories thought lost and suddenly brought sailing back into harbour. Memories that burst prow-forward into sight again, and one is once more a young, earnest seeker after loveliness, scrawling away to capture a breath of beauty—beauty that survives, even now, through faded ink on faded pages.

With the book came a note written in John's positive hand, with the " r " and the " e " always written as capitals, no matter what their place in the word, and the " I " strong, forceful and egotistically dynamic.

This was his letter. I reproduce it in full:

Nov. 14

My dear Ralph,

A voice from the past—almost the dead past. You may have heard that I was gravely ill. As a result I had to tidy up things and in going through mountains of debris found two things, one a surprise, which gave me great pleasure.

The first was a charming letter you sent me after my mother died ten years ago. The other I enclose. God knows how it has survived thirty years!

I read it with blurred vision, I must confess. And I am sure

it will give you nostalgic pleasure to have the commonplace
book back again after virtually a lifetime.

It is unlikely that we shall meet again, so I now wish you
Goodbye and a long and pleasant journey in the happy up-
lands.

Sincerely,
John S. Mather

He read it with blurred vision and I with tears falling. Not
so much for the book and the lifetime of living gone, but for
him, John. In one letter all the exterior sham of hardness and
toughness had vanished. Between the words was the spectre-
thin boy grabbing eagerly at life, seeking to impress by his
physical strength and finally impressing, without question, by
his academic brilliance and his great journalism, his professional skill at his adopted trade.

If I had not known it before I knew then that John's life
was a sham of looking masterful and acting dictatorially. He
was a boy as I was; a weak groping man as I was; a soft, sentimental soul stirred to hide this weakness from the world.

He had been curt to me too. And bossy. Abrupt and off-
hand. But now he was as he really was. And I wept for him.

He had always been a hypochondriac. Friends of mine on
the *Express* said that he opened almost every conversation
with "How do I look?" Like the two psychoanalysts who
met and one said to the other: "Good morning, how are
you? And how am I?" John was always worried about his
health. He had good reason to be. His family history was
death. His own breakdown at seventeen had left him morbid
and introspective, forever fearing another and final breakdown. His younger brother had died before John was twenty.
He was the last surviving male member of what had once been
a large family. He worried continuously about himself.

Yet he grew fat. He delighted in his bulk. It was thinness
he feared: the thinness which sometimes points to tuberculosis. Life is full of ironies. He had feared T.B. all his life and he
finally went down with a coronary brought about to some extent by his fondness for flesh and the good things in life that
put it on—rich food, rich wine, rich living.

I hoped that John was worrying unduly. Other men had
survived a coronary; some two or even three. Why not John?

Thus cheered, I went to see him in hospital. He knew I was coming but, at the bedside, asked me to leave as he wanted to sleep. He had dosed himself with sleeping tablets.

I had travelled nearly thirty miles to see him and when I got to his bed he asked me to leave.

I could have been annoyed. I was, for a short while. But I had a chat with the Sister and I heard that he was a very sick man. He had muscular distrophy and diabetes.

His lungs had been scarred by T.B., his heart by a coronary thrombosis and now he had muscular distrophy and diabetes.

But Sister was not without hope. She told me that Britain's finest doctors were taking a special interest in John. They recognised a brilliant mind when they chatted to him. They liked him. One of them was a close friend of John's and had been for years. During his span at the *Express* John had moved in exalted circles. While I was there the country's leading Professor of Economics telephoned.

Sister was a little bit angry with John. He was a difficult patient. He had decided that he could cure himself by what he described as Sleep Therapy. He had obviously read about it in the obscure medical publications he was always studying. He was before his time. For only recently I saw an article in our most distinguished medical journal on the benefits of this very method of treatment.

John had managed, somehow or other, to hide sleeping pills from the nursing staff. And when he was in pain he'd dope himself and sleep for days on end, waking up only to take more tablets.

She was sure visitors brought them. Some of them were doctors, friends of John. Maybe . . .? Or chemists who called, perhaps . . .? Or someone. She couldn't have visitors searched.

When next I rang the hospital John had been discharged. That same evening the telephone rang and there was John, sounding happy enough, apologising for having sent me away from his bed. Perhaps I'd go and see him.

I went. He lived in a council flat on a pleasant enough estate on the heights of Dulwich.

He greeted me cordially. He looked fine. His beard was trimmed in Edwardian dandy fashion. His sports suit was not out of the multiple tailors.

We chatted. Suddenly he wanted to hear about my mother,

my sisters, my brothers. Suddenly, it seemed, he knew that he had neglected to keep in touch with them.

He told me about his illness. The doctors were hopeful they could slow down the progress of the muscular distrophy while keeping the diabetes under control. John knew as much as any doctor about his illnesses and their treatment. He told me about his Sleep Therapy. He had a store of sleeping pills, gathered from many sources. Sometimes he would sleep for a week on end. He was convinced that he could best the disease by this form of treatment. In sleep, he explained, the diseased part of the nervous system and the body were getting the rest they could not get in wakefulness. Nature had a chance to go to work and heal its own shortcomings. It was very convincing. John was a very convincing man.

The only thing that bothered me, and then only slightly, was his expressed fear that neighbours wanted his flat. That they were trying to turn him out. There was a long waiting list for these very agreeable premises with their delightful situation and John believed that some neighbours were conniving at his tenancy being ended.

I thought nothing more about it. We parted and I promised to look him up again.

Two days later I heard that John had been taken to hospital in a diabetic coma. I rushed to the hospital. John was sitting up in bed this time and seemed full of life. He laughed. Someone had broken into his flat when they saw the milk bottles piling up outside and had found him so soundly asleep that he could not be roused. Diabetic coma his aunt fanny, he said. Sleeping tablets, that was all.

He discharged himself a few days later.

He'd ring me up every night and we'd chat. He was closer to me now than he'd ever been, even as a boy. He seemed somehow dependent on me. It was so unlike him. He had always carried himself with such pride and aloofness, never caring a damn about what people thought of him, always maintaining that if he were judged only by his ability and the work he was doing, he would earn respect. It was true. He was respected; even when he was most hated. You had to respect his genius.

One evening he didn't sound so good. He begged me to come as soon as possible. I went to his flat the very next day.

I have never known such a shambles. The front door was splintered as though it had been forced. The lock was smashed and the door was ajar. I walked in. The corridor was full of fluff and bits of broken glass, paper, tins, rubbish. The untidiness thickened as I got into the living-room. This was a mess. Feathers lay thick on everything. Paper and rubbish littered the floor. Two chairs were upturned. I moved into the bedroom and was revolted by the sight that met my eyes. Feathers were everywhere like snow. The room was full of dust and dirt. Furniture was lying all over the place. Piles of books littered the floor. The phone was off the hook—John always removed it when he was practising Sleep Therapy—and the bedclothes, dirty and stained, were half on the floor. John was fast asleep in a thick messy bed, grey with unwashing, stained with tea, food, soup and urine.

He woke as I entered as though he had been expecting me. He asked me to make him a cup of tea.

I made him fourteen cups. *Fourteen.* I have never seen such thirst. He knew what I was thinking.

" Yes. It's the diabetes playing me up."

Could I help in any way? Indeed I could. Could I tidy up the mess? I removed my jacket, rolled up my sleeves and began to work. I mopped and dusted and went down on my hands and knees wiping with a wet cloth and some detergent I had found in the kitchen. I vacuum-cleaned. I picked up innumerable pieces of fluff, almost a bagful of feathers. I set the furniture to rights.

I was working for four hours, mostly on my hands and knees. Any housewife would have been proud of me that day.

Between whiles John had got up, flung a worn dressing-robe round him and, sitting down, told me the story of the shambles.

Someone had got in and torn the flat apart. In trying to remonstrate with the someone, in the dark, John had been hit on the head. He showed me an ugly gash on his temple.

It sounded plausible. But what was all that broken glass doing all over the place? I asked the question.

" Don't you see, Ralph? They want to kill me. They mixed up all my tablets (he had dozens of bottles of different pills) and then, when I woke up and guessed what they were doing, they deliberately smashed them after knocking me out. They want to get rid of me. To get this flat. But I'm not done yet . . ."

It didn't make sense. I asked if he'd sent for the police. He hadn't. But the neighbours had. The police thought he wasn't telling the truth. His doctor? That fathead sided with the police too. Would I do him a favour? Please! Would I ask Doctor Anon to see him. Doctor Anon was a mutual friend of ours. We had been at school together. He and John had kept up a desultory kind of friendship over the years. Sometimes they had met. I said I would contact Dr. A.

John was feeling tired. The flat was at least somewhat tidier if not as spick and span as it could have been. I emptied John's chamber pot, helped him into bed and in a trice he was asleep. I had a feeling he had taken more pills under my very nose.

I let myself out and started down the stairs.

On the landing below a woman beckoned to me. She was a neat, motherly soul, well-spoken, friendly.

Would I take a cup of tea with her? I did. She told me that John was going mad. He had smashed up the flat himself. All the neighbours had heard the shemozzle. He had broken his bottles of pills, flung the furniture about, taken pillows from the bed and pounded them against the walls till the air was thick with fluff and feathers. She had gone in and settled him down. It transpired, though I had to question her on this before I found the answer, that she had fed John when he was first sick and nursed him and cleaned the flat. She was sorry for him. I knew she was telling the truth. She was a good woman. Now he wouldn't let her near him. Or anyone. The sight of anyone within yards of him made John violent. What did I suggest? She knew who I was. John had often talked of me. With affection and regard.

I told her I was going to contact a mutual doctor friend and that he would let us know the best course to pursue. She was very grateful. She was truly worried for and sorry about John. When I got home I immediately rang Doctor Anon and he promised to help. For old time's sake.

He telephoned the very next day. He said he had been to see John and John was quite definitely mentally deranged. Possibly from taking pills; probably because the muscular distrophy was affecting brain centres. John had asked him for a supply of sleeping pills.

" You do understand why I can't let him have them?" Doctor Anon asked.

Of course I understood. And I told Doctor Anon so.

I asked him what course should be taken.

Doctor Anon thought John needed treatment—institutional treatment. He suggested that John's own doctor be informed and he would be willing to add his own signature to that of the local doctor.

" You're not going to certify him?" I was horrified.

Doctor Anon explained that John would not be kept in hospital a day longer than was necessary. But he did need mental as opposed to physical treatment.

He, too, thought that John, in a fit of madness, had smashed his own furniture, banged the pillows around, broken the bottles of pills; and that he had fallen and hit his head and had passed out. The idea of intruders was too far fetched. There was no evidence for it. I said I would be in favour of anything that helped John, that might improve his condition. But I would not let it rest if he were victimised.

" You don't think I'd be a party to that?" Of course I knew Doctor Anon would not. He had John's interests at heart too. So I left the matter in his hands.

Three days later I was informed that John was in a mental hospital somewhere in Surrey.

I went to see him. Through corridors as grim as a prison, past gaping, dazed and out-of-this-world patients sitting on benches and looking forlorn, through paint-scarred, toilet-type doors I went, and the further I went the more depressing and decayed the outlook grew till one got the impression that this was a kind of undecorated hell, a place where people and things stagnated and rotted.

He was in a cell. A cell. A stone room with a high, out-of-reach window and a heavy door with a grilled peephole cut high in it. He was lying on his bed but rose, without effort it seemed, on seeing me and greeted me heartily enough.

I set down the cigarettes I had brought and we talked. John insisted that he was there for physical treatment. He pointed to a foot which had been bruised and was now suppurating. His condition made any wound worse than it might have been in normal people. The healing process was slow. Danger of infection high.

He said he had been burgled again and his flat ransacked. That he had woken up, gone to tackle the intruders and hit his foot against a chest of drawers. He had fallen, blacked out, and awakened in the ambulance taking him to this place.

When I had been told by someone in authority at the mental hospital that John was there, I had been told, too, that he had had to be taken by force, resisting arrest until quietened.

Poor John.

He was optimistic and rational enough. The only signs of mental instability were when he motioned me, putting finger to lips, to speak in a whisper. They, the guards outside, listened in and reported everything he said.

"I'm well enough for a man who is dying," he said.

"We're all dying, John," I said.

"But some," he said, "are dying faster than others."

He called: "Guard, guard!" A male nurse entered. John asked to be helped to dress. Then, with a stick as crutch, we went out into the grounds. The grounds were pretty and the summer sun lent peace and quiet to the shady walks and flowered gardens.

The only sign of an unreal world was in the people who passed: people who talked to themselves, shied away from you as you approached or who, sat on benches staring into nowhere, and looked at you with a pathetic, helpless, frightened look. You knew they were not sane.

As we walked I was encouraged by John's mobility. He began to use his stick as a walking stick and strode purposefully forward. We sat down. Out into the walled garden came a group of inmates with three nurses in attendance.

Why three nurses? I wanted to know. They were the dangerous prisoners, John told me. Some played amongst themselves, running round one another in circles; others walked backwards and forwards towards each other in a monotony of aimlessness. Some merely sat on the grass and stared. Others walked alone, the sad ones, the frightened ones. It was like being in a bad dream. Once again I had the feeling I had had as a child, the feeling that the years had tucked away, right away into the forgotten parts of my mind, the feeling that everything was happening at a crawling pace: that actions had been slowed down by some sort of an unnatural inner lens and

N

that what I was looking at was slow motion film. There was an indescribable lethargy about everything, a sense of time standing still, a foreboding and sinister unreality. Once again it was a summer day's nightmare I was living in.

We talked about John Macadam who had just died. John had been a great friend of John's. He was a fine writer who used to do a feature in the old *News Chronicle*, had written a book about his experiences in the R.A.F. and had, after the war, written the sports feature for the *Daily Express*. A spell of illness, lung trouble, had left him out of the public and press eye and in his last years he had been just a sports reporter eking out a living. It was a sad waste of a rare talent.

John told me how he and Macadam used to go walking through Devon and Cornwall, of their close understanding and the great times they had had. Macadam was about John's age when he died and John said sadly: " He's gone to warm a seat for me in Hell."

" You know," he said to me, " I can't complain. I've lived a crowded hour of glorious life. I've squeezed more out of living than a dozen ordinary men do in longer lifetimes. I've had women by the bellyful, some of the loveliest women you could imagine; drunk every kind of drink in every conceivable place at every conceivable time; travelled; seen the world; lived it up; foregone sleep; laughed a lot; loved occasionally. When you think of the way the odds were stacked against me from the start, I can't grumble at the way things have turned out . . ."

And then, for the first and only time, John said something which let me look deep down inside this complex man and see something of the real person behind all the artificial veneer.

" I didn't want people to know my background. You used to think I was ashamed of it—the East End, the buildings, the dirt, the poverty. I wasn't ashamed, merely trying to forget in order to build a life that could ignore one's bad start and still sing. And I've sung. I've beaten that bad beginning. But I always remembered the old days. And I want you to know that though you may have thought me churlish and ungrateful, I've always remembered your dear mother and what she did for me—I've loved her like my second mother all the days of my life—and I've remembered your brothers and your sisters; and though I didn't ever thank them, the thanks have always been there, believe me. And you, Ralph, you've turned out the best friend a man ever had—and all along, even when I was moving away from you, I knew this was so. I want you to know that. It isn't easy, you understand, for me to say this. I won't say it again . . ."

I left him sitting there, enjoying the sunlight. It was the last time I was ever to see him alive again.

He rang me a couple of days later to say he was back in the flat. He mentioned that his Public Assistance grant was barely enough to keep him in cigarettes. Fortunately, my sister had sent him some. Bless her. I had told her about John and without any prompting she had got in touch with him and had written to him. He told me he had received a marvellous and uplifting letter from her; that he was delighted to know my old mother was still hanging on to life. It was wonderful and uplifting that all the people who had helped him in the old, old days were the ones who were trying to help him now.

I hadn't realised that John was living on Public Assistance. I immediately sat down and wrote a letter to Lord Beaverbrook. I told him of John's plight.

Within a few days John rang me up gleefully to say that the *Express* had suddenly remembered him, sent a director down to see him and given him a hundred pounds. I let John think the idea had come from them. But I was grateful to the *Express*. I had not thought my letter to the Beaver would get such rapid action. It proved to me that even newspapers have a heart and from that time on I have thought most kindly of the paper. It was a nice gesture. They didn't *have* to do anything. Good for them.

And then, suddenly, I heard he was in hospital again and I rushed around and when I got there I found he had died. He had had a second coronary.

We had been friends as boys, had—apart from rare contact —lost touch when we were young men, and had found friendship again in our forties. His sending me the autograph album had inspired *No Tears in Aldgate*, a book he liked very much and, thus, because of the way *No Tears* was well received, this book as its follow-up. Without John, without that autograph album, the old days would not have come back in such fine line as they had, unbidden, spurring me to rethink and remember. The " commonplace book " as John had called it had inspired two books forty years on. And neither book, then, was written to " cash in " on the fashionable world of the East End, Miss Reviewer for *Punch*!

All his life John had been struggling. He was born with the dice weighted heavily against him. He inherited sickness. But he fought. He fought life every inch of the way, and he needed to be tough, for it was a tough battle. Nothing came easily to him. When I see the young pop stars of today who beckon for success to come running I am white with heat at the unfair tricks life plays. Girls who shake on their top notes and admit, after they have achieved success—*after*, mind you; not before—that they can't sing, make thousands of pounds a week. Boys with a mental ability so far below John's that they are not fit to lick his dead boots made money and found success when John was using every ounce of his considerable talent to stay afloat in a grim world.

Where have all our standards gone? Where our sense of discernment, our judgement, our scale of values? We are all being conned. The public is taking its biggest cuckolding ever. Untalented young men and women are being foisted on us by shrewd publicity and we are being caught up in the sham. The youngsters, the stupid, the loutish, the unmanly, now representing the biggest spending section of the population, are so in control that we are letting immaturity rule us and inexperience guide us.

What a monstrous state of affairs we have come to. People who do not know how to live are telling those, who have suffered to learn, what to wear, what to listen to, how to dance, how to sing, act, breathe. How to become famous without talent.

Commercial interests, sponsoring the cult of the young and the ignorant, have caught up the conformists—about ninety-nine per cent of the population—in the charade and everyone is doing what the young people do.

Remember Browning? In my autograph album?

> Does he paint? He fain would write a poem—
> Does he write? He fain would paint a picture.

Now they don't fain it, they feign it. Does he write? He paints too. And acts. Does he paint? He writes and sings and gets screened on the box so that a captive audience may be captivated by what they believe, or are conned to believe, is talent.

A man writes music, so he publishes poetry. And it sells. A girl sings, O so badly, stretching and screeching and trembling and shaking and quivering over the high notes, a thin little voice out of a thin little girl, and she becomes a hit selling mod gear or is even put into the lead in a West End production. Some are nice, plain girls (and boys) without ability. Others are cheap little tarts or effeminate upstarts. All sup blue. *Who fished the murex up?*

What is happening to us?

Where is talent?

What price effort and soul-scarring struggles? Poor young Keats. Poor old John.

Had he been born twenty years later he could have taken up, say photography, and made an easy life for himself. Or mouthed into a mike with the best of them. He looked the part they're all trying to look with his Edwardian dandy look and his proud eye and his authoritative manner. The only difference is: he had talent and he worked at it.

John fought life from the moment he could think. And he beat it. What a fierce struggle it all was and how much more rewarding the rewards must have been for him because they didn't come, as they come to today's sham starlets, easily.

People didn't like him. But you needed to know him. And I only really got to know him too late. Inside that uncompromising sick body there was a generous mind and a very warm heart. Inside that brilliant brain there was more goodness than onlookers recognised. He had never really forgotten his beginnings or his friends.

Dear John. Friend of my youth. No more we'll tire the sun with talking and send him down the sky. Farewell my old Carian guest.

He was cremated. There was hardly anybody present to witness his farewell to the land of the living. The *Express* sent a representative. Doctor Anon came. My sister. Some distant relatives of John's. About a dozen people in all to say goodbye to this man.

A handful of grey ashes at rest. Peace at last.

And a tattered autograph album to link me forever to the boy who was my dearest friend.

WE DECIDED the time had come for us to leave Broughton
Buildings and shake the dust of the East End off our feet and
the smell of it from our nostrils.

There were worse areas in which to live. At that time Bermondsey, Wapping, Rotherhithe, the Old Kent Road, Poplar,
West Ham—particularly the Canning Town area, Shoreditch,
Hoxton and Shadwell were far worse places to live in. They
were real slums. So were Islington and Canonbury and Camden Town.

Now, of course, parts of Islington and Camden Town, even
Aldgate itself, have become fashionable.

It makes me laugh. What is there about age and its attendant decrepitude that suddenly transforms what was once ugly
into what is now lovely? I am not saying that some of the
little squares in the Islington area are not pretty, but they
were always so. And the houses are pretty old, too. But Vic-
toriana and sham Georgiana are enjoying a vogue. And a
vogue makes everything all right.

I wouldn't live in one of those tall Victorian monstrosities
if you gave it to me. A friend of mine, a film director, married
a very attractive model. They put their two attractive bodies
into a narrow Victorian house in Kensington. The house
would have been rated a slum dwelling in any other part of
London but in the Royal Borough it was a fashionable house.
They lived quietly until the baby was born. Then, with the
baby up six flights of stairs and the living-room downstairs,
they and a succession of nannies had the job of climbing endless stairs. When the nannies threw in the towel the couple had
to cope alone. Up and down, up and down. There was damp
in the basement and the place required an abnormal amount
of heat. The stairs wore them out. They began to fight. She
wasn't geared to cope with such a house. He loved his com-

fort. They parted. Each to a modern, no-stairs flat.

Fashion is a sham. How often, however, does it lead even the intelligent to stupid conformity. The houses in the now-fashionable squares of Islington and Camden are still surrounded by some of the grimmest property and ugliest scenery in London. Some houses are big, their rooms amply proportioned, but they are set on stairs at all sorts of irregular intervals; there is no real comfort in such living and a ridiculous ignoring of the fact that modernity, even if you don't consider it beautiful, has made life easier.

Age in itself is not, *per se*, beautiful. Another friend of mine collects Victorian pieces of china made to resemble famous faces and places. There is Lord Kitchener, Baden Powell, the Albert Memorial, Tower Bridge, St. Paul's, Westminster Abbey, Victoria herself, Albert, and the past historic too in the shapes of Nelson, Wellington, Shakespeare. All hideously ugly. Unshapely, unlovely. Lacking a likeness, lacking proportion, lacking grace. Yet, I am told, these pieces are now collectors' treasures. When I was young we used to have them on the stall and practically give them away. Some of the smaller items fell out of the lucky bags, filled with sherbet, that we used to buy. They had no worth, no value, no artistic merit then. Why have they suddenly become respectable?

The worship of the old for old time's sake fills me with nausea. I can see that pieces of pottery dug out of the ground where they have lain buried since the Romans left Britain, or even before that, have historic significance; but when people fawn over their symmetry and stroke the outlines, I feel like puking. Many are so badly made. The work of a poor craftsman in 1067 doesn't become good work because it lies in the ground nine hundred years.

I have seen vases so preciously handled, so fawned over as beautiful, so praised for their loveliness that were so out of shape, out of true, out of grace that they looked like amateurish imitations of works of art. Yet they were being regarded as things of beauty.

There are some very famous paintings, Italian mostly, representing Virgin and Child which, for me, are always spoiled by the cherubic representation of the child Jesus; supposed to be an infant, and looking for all the world like a mis-shapen dwarf, an ugly gnome. Some of the world's most treasured religious paintings come into this category. They are works of art. But the children in most of them are repulsive. I understand that it was difficult, even in those days to get a young child to pose; that a new-born babe, which is what many of them depict, cannot be made to hold the same posture and stance; but if they were truly one hundred per cent beautiful these paintings would not be marred by such monstrous children. For me, then, these priceless treasures fall short of perfection.

I am fussy, you see. My long immersion in turgid waters has taught me the value of limpidity and lucidity. I look for the light that shines through the darkness, listen for the still small voice in the storm.

Age can be beautiful but it is not necessarily so. It is often ugly.

The East End can be beautiful but not if you know it as I do. Then it is largely unlovely.

So we decided to leave the unlovely East End. And we threw a party. Our rooms were crowded with dozens of people. There was an endless round of tea and sandwiches, piles of fruit and cakes. And some wine for the privileged.

Everyone came. John Mather was there, a young man verging towards genius, with the mark of death over him; pale, thin, tough. How he talked that night. How he laughed. It was the last time my family was ever to see him. Shorty, tall, handsome, debonair making passes at Wendy Tuppness. Roger Bagehot and Alice embracing in the narrow scullery. Solly Shumer called Shtumer because he stuttered. Abrams, the bookmaker, whom we had long since forgiven. Gordon the mad Highlander in full regalia, with his pipes tucked underneath his arm. Uncle Lotting sang. My Zaida grew red faced with much wine drinking. My Booba made endless cups of tea and cut fresh sandwiches as fast as they were being eaten. Shlomka was there, big, burly, bearded, and his henchman Itzik. *Why don't you shut up?* And his wife who was saying precisely that to him all evening. And Sammy Cockeye and Manny, blind, and his wife Doreen and kid brother Jackie.

We had made many friends in the Buildings. There was a warmth and unaffected kindliness in the East End in those days the like of which I have never met again. In adversity, in poverty, in the day-to-day struggle for existence big things were born: humanity, tolerance, togetherness. There they were, all together, in the shape of people—the men, women and children who have filled these pages.

My first love, Wendy Tuppness, who became a film star and went to Hollywood and married a millionaire and died world famous. Alice, who became a respectable barmaid and died serving drinks in her pub when a buzz-bomb hit it. The tailor who invented a rotary iron and went into gowns and became a millionaire. Three future millionaires under one roof. One prostitute. One sex crazy schoolboy. Two doctors. And a writer.

Looking back on it all I sometimes think I was the only one who stayed alive who didn't make money. Had I written my books some ten years later than I did, I might have been rich. I would have been caught up in the fashionable East End of the post-war. Back to fashion again. Ah well, never the time and the place and the loved one—my writing—all together.

We did not go to bed that night. The noise we made kept everyone in the tall tenement awake and so they eventually found their way into the two rooms, bare of furniture now—it was all downstairs in the entrance porchway awaiting removal—but overflowing with people.

Bleary-eyed and hoarse we saw our last East End dawn and were much too drunk with excitement to greet it. Toasts were drunk to Absent Friends: to Morry Leshy, Paddy Rourke, Doctor Deacon, Father Gregory and even to Morry's mother, the Hatpin Woman who had languished in prison and died there.

Everyone kissed everyone else.

And then the removal van had arrived and the furniture was bundled into it and we all got into the back of the van and to a street lined with cheering people, to wavings from windows and greetings from passers-by, to Good Lucks from dustmen, postmen, policemen, bookies, barrow-boys, stallholders and office goers on their way to work we began to move off.

The van moved away out of Goolden Street towards fresh fields and pastures newer, greener, more fashionable, but never as friendly as the East End that had sheltered us for so many years.

We moved away and took our love of the East End with us as we went. And we never forgot it.

Epilogue

I WENT back to Broughton Buildings.

The going back was not inspired by me. But, after a quarter of a century of forgetting, I had to go back.

And I went.

Reality is a fusion of particles of illusion. Each separate flash of living is seen through rose or rainbow or rue-coloured spectacles and the whole is a distorted vision of actuality and existence. Authenticity is a chameleon which takes its varying hues from the beliefs of the beholder. Colour exists only in the mind's eye. Even the scientists admit this.

James Agate flattered me by dubbing me " at once both realist and romantic ". Realist I am not. I don't tell the truth as others see it: only as I see it. Truth is believing; seeing is not.

So, no one can recreate my youth but me. No one can recreate the environment of that youth and the years of that youth and the agonies and ecstasies of that youth, but me. The East End in the years before the war exists for others too, but not in the same way as it exists for me. We are all of us eye witnesses to the same period of living and we all have our different versions of it.

I don't call that nostalgia. I may have more nostalgia than others for the lost days of my youth. Perhaps I am more aware than most that they will never come again: not the days, but the youth itself. There is no future in looking back. By the same token, there is no past in looking forward. Man is a composite of all the days of his life. All experience is an arch where through gleams that untravelled world whose margin fades forever and forever as one moves. No man dare say: I am now, as of this moment—nothing else matters.

Everything matters. When I weep for the days that were I am weeping for the people who were, for those whose death diminished me, whose growing old saddened me. For people not places. For souls not slums.

I weep for life. For life which grows stiff and feeble and frail. And when I laugh it must be for the joys that were worth laughing about. And how one laughed when the world was young!

The past made me what I am: good, bad or indifferent. I can no more dismiss it than the present can dismiss history. Let those who can, do.

Stay with me, then, days full of the merriment of dancing spring. Westwind-blown on aureate clouds let memory come singing. Let the dead arise. Let me hear happiness and see laughter holding both its sides.

If this is nostalgia, okay—I'm nostalgic. The dread of the Englishman to show sentimentality in any shape is a ridiculous fear. It makes him so much less of a man. He needs a drink to open his lips and the false atmosphere of the pub before he can laugh uninhibitedly. He is as tight as a fully wound spring. Beer is the oil that releases the tension. Or gin. Or whisky. Devoid of that overt warmth that naturally opens the heart of strangers the Englishman has foisted upon himself the myth that ice cold reserve is an admirable quality. What's admirable about it? What's so wrong about the world knowing when and why and how you're in sorrow or in pain? People would be so much more willing to sympathise if they only knew *when* sympathy was needed, or if they felt they could display it without being made to feel embarrassed and foolish.

Life in the cold climate is all right for the unfeeling, the stony-hearted, the public schoolers who are taught the false value of the stiff upper lip, the mothers who were proud when their sons were killed in war. Proud. What was there to be proud about? Better that the tears should have come in unceasing paroxysms of grief than that the lips should quiver only so slightly.

Let the tears flow like fountains by the gates of Bathsheba, let the heart worn on the sleeve palpitate with sighs. Let floods of feeling overwhelm the soul. Weep, my people. Weep. By the gates of Babylon we sat down and wept. We hung our harps on the willows and the willows wept. Weeping is more than laughter. In weeping is the immortality of

music, the plaintive notes of the violin, the passion of the
'cello, the true beauty of Beethoven and Bach, the ineffable
sadness of Keats, the greatness that made great men. And then
laughter, when it comes, is real and true and when someone
laughs you hear God chuckling.

And the rain falls on quiet streets and the flowers drip
pearls of dew and from a world of hills the blue misted Tyr-
hennian clouds float together into a mauveness of storm and
the tempest tossed waves beat high. And the heart weeps for
lostnesses, so many people lost and by the people forgotten.
And then laughter comes like tinkling rills, like slivers of
pendant glass chinking in a breeze and in that laughter that
comes after tears is the real heart of man.

And balls to your sham pubs and your sham laughter and
your striving to appear merry. O what deceit is there. What
sadness in such laughter. What phoniness.

In tears has the world wrought its greatness. In the agony
of Warsaw, in the assassination of Ghandi, in the crucifixion
of Christ. Out of sadness and sorrow, out of suffering and
despair have come the big things of mankind. In the sobbing
of the strings and the moan of the woodwinds is great music
born: in melodic grace and heart-moving episode is there
lyricism and *weltschmerz*.

Laughter has its place. But so much of it is sham. I will
trade all the laughter of all the world's comics for one deliri-
ously happy chuckle of a child. I would trade all the laughter
in the world for the slim volume of Tennyson's " In
Memoriam "; all the jokes that ever were for the sweet sadness of my brother Ben singing " Brown Bird," for John
McCormack singing " The Old House ".

The world walks around with smiles on its lips. Shallow
quips and hollow jests. Empty words that lack depth and feeling and soul. Life is a veneer that shines with gloss. But the
veneer is laughter thin.

So many people never think. They have no deep thoughts.
They think they think. There was a time when I thought
everyone searched his soul as I do, looked deep into his heart,
wondered why we were here and what we were supposed to
do; and then I realised that some people can't and most people
won't think serious thoughts. Enough for them the sound of
revelry, the false approach, the mundane, the trite, the com-

monplace; or the pseudo intellectual air that considers itself so superior to mass thinking and mass living, and—reading the classy Sunday papers—thinks it therefore justifies its merito-cratic conceit.

Who can look into the heart of his brother? Ah, but who tries? The world has ears but it hears not, eyes but it sees not. It hears what it wants to hear and sees what it wants to see. And try as I do I cannot see into the heart of man and under-stand. It is given to me to understand only me.

I have tried to look back. Not, may I say again, with nos-talgia; not because I would ever want those days to come again. But the people are worth remembering even if the place should be forgotten.

When I was seventeen it was a very good year. It was a good year for friends, for warmth, for understanding, for growing. It was a good year because it will never come again. I was young and the world was green. So it was when I was seven. And all the ten years in between. And, after that, life caught up with me. It's never been that good since.

Back there in the slum of Broughton's Buildings the world was green and Aldgate smiled on me.

When you come to think of it life's absurd. Even if one ful-fils every dream—and so few of us do—one does it at a cost of life itself. Who would not change his millions for a chance to be young again? Life's absurd because one only really lives it before one has begun to live.

Maybe Dave and John and Morry and Paddy got the best out of living after all. There wasn't a lot more to come, not of pure unadulterated ecstasy. The glory drops from youth. The bright day wanes into slow twilight. The art of living for the moment is lost. And living for tomorrow—what is that but the end?

But life is for the living. Time will not be halted. So it must be gotten on with. And Time says: say now your fond fare-wells. *Au revoir* Youth. 'Bye Broughton Buildings. *Auf wied-ersehen* Goolden Street. *Arrivederci* Aldgate. Till the moun-tains join the dance and all the trees of the forest cha-cha-cha to the music of the spheres and the sunshine of the world's smiles floods over all its people. Till we all meet again, some-time, somewhere. Till the thirteenth day of never and beyond, and all that jazz.

I have gone back. I have never really gone away. I am forever young, forever alive in a youth that was real, earnest, agonising, painful and joyful. It is my great gift that I was born where I was born amongst the people who were there when I was there. To come back to them out of this place of shame and deceit is to know something of the mystery of being. Ralph L. Finn is become Peter Pan.

Nothing is every destroyed. No shadow is cast in vain. There must be some far-off divine event to which the whole creation moves. It must all make sense. For me it has always made sense. For I have never forgotten. And I am never likely to forget.

*   *   *

And so, after twenty-five years, I came back to Broughton Buildings. *No Tears In Aldgate* had been welcomed and the television people wanted to film me in my own home.

It was a freezing February day. On the only remaining tenement the icicles hung from the wall. The building was a dirtier grey than I remembered it. The playground seemed so much smaller than I thought. The enchantment distance had lent to the view fell fast away. I was ashamed of the place and of myself for ever having lived there.

In the areas Indians were hanging washing. That, at least, was an improvement. The men and women I saw looked cleaner and neater than we had been; but that was no surprise —the Indians are a far cleaner race than the British.

I met two or three men, now middle aged, who had been boys when I was a boy. They had never moved from the Buildings. Had survived the bombs which tore down two-thirds of the pile, had married and brought their wives to the Buildings and their children were now playing in the playground. They had missed nothing. They still thought there was no place like Broughton Buildings. They worked in Petticoat Lane, in Goolden or Wentworth Street, they were close to their work, they loved the markets, the market atmosphere, the herded proximity of masses of people. And they were happy. Had I really gone any farther than they? Had I achieved anything more? Had I found something in life that they had not? It could not have been content, for they were content. It could not have been happiness, for they were happy.

What I had found was the ecstasy of sadness. The sweet slow melancholic agony of knowing suffering and, by anti-thesis, being made aware of different shapes of happiness; so that my joy, when it came, was fuller, richer, riper than any they could experience. My dimensions were different. Mine was a psychedelic world where colour rioted and poetry sang and music filled me with a sense of God.

They were simple souls. The daily round, the common task furnished all they had to ask. I had yearned for more. And had paid the price. Sweet content may have golden slumbers. I would settle for my insomnia. I did not really want to be like them. But I did envy them their unambition, their easy satisfaction, their simple faith.

I walked around with the television cameras following me. I looked at a notice which warned that games were forbidden. It had been there when I was a boy. The same rules and the same non-observance.

I was sad and heavy hearted. The Building had not really changed. I had changed. This was no place for me.

Then I saw some kids playing in the yard. There, there was a boy with a ball at his feet and he looked just like Paddy Rourke had done when he was learning how to tie a ball to his toes. He had the same lissom grace, the same slight build and fair frail look. And there, standing apart, was a dark thin lad with large luminous eyes—Morry Leshy come to life. And addressing a group of youngsters a stern, pale faced lad who might have been John; and a tall, good-looking kid who could have been Shorty. A big tousle-headed boy was chas-ing some girls. Roger Bagehot in the miniature. And there, climbing the spiked railings to retrieve a ball, was a sickly-looking bespectacled lad who showed agility one did not ex-pect from so weedy a specimen. And that was me. I watched him and saw myself when young.

Then an old woman came by, shuffling, bent, wrinkled. And my heart missed a beat. I gazed at the old woman and had to hold myself back from running to her and embracing her. For there, to the life, was my grandmother, my Booba, the immortal unchanging indestructible perennial picture of old age in all its tender beauty.

Then I knew I had had enough. The street outside was full of bearded old men who looked like my Zaida and the more I stood there the more I felt that the world had swung back on its axis and time had retraced its wild spinning and I was back among the men and women and children I knew. People did not change.

To make the illusion complete a young bird, just like Alice, stood at a tenement entrance and winked at me and I looked too long at her and her cherried mouth opened and she dearied me in Alice's mutilated accent and I saw that she, too, was no more than seventeen.

That was the end. For I had the selfsame feelings of fear that I used to have as a boy; that she was unclean. Only now, as a man, everything was unclean. The whole place was sordid and disgusting.

I went out of the yard and walked slowly towards the spot where we had lived. It was flat. A car park. You would never know, by looking at it, how many lives had been spent on that spot, how much living had had its beginning and end in the space where cars stood like herds of silent wild animals at a desert water hole.

Gone was the house now and gone were the people. The children were scattered. The old folks were dead. Many were dead. And all of us were dying, as everyone is dying from the moment of birth.

I saw again the days when we were young. I lived for a brief moment the childhood days. In a flash of perception I had about me, for a brief span, all the dear ones gone.

The man behind the camera said " Get moving . . . please !"

It was time to be moving.

Time to pass on . . .